**S-Factor**

## *Salvation Is...*

"All about Jesus! With salvation, God draws us to Him. We do not seek salvation. It chooses us."

— **Randy Horton**,
Director, Good News Connection

"God's best gift bestowed to me through the suffering and death of His dear son, Jesus. It's victory over the devil's plan."

— **Bridget Turay**,
Certified Nursing Assistant

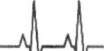

"Acceptance of Christ's payment and dismissal of charges against me for my sins. It's bridging the gap between myself and God and bringing us again into communion."

— **Dedric Carter**,
Child of God

"Opening my heart to Jesus allowing Him in so we can commune."

— **Vivienne Morana**,
Teacher

**Bridgette Bastien**

S-Factor

# S-Factor

## Prayer SAVED My Life
### A SERIES BY Bridgette Bastien

**Bridgette Bastien**

Unless otherwise indicated, all Bible references are taken from the New King James Version®. Copyright©1982 by Thomas Nelson. Used by permission. All rights reserved.

Scripture quotations from The Authorized (King James) Version. Rights in the Authorized Version in the United Kingdom are vested in the Crown. Reproduced by permission of the Crown's patentee, Cambridge University Press.

All the stories related in this book are true, but most of the names have been changed or omitted to protect the privacy of the people mentioned.

Book cover designed by **Raman Bhardwaj**
Interior page elements designed by **Bridgette Bastien**

**S-Factor: Prayer Saved My Life**

Copyright ©2020 Bridgette Bastien. All rights reserved. This book or any portion thereof may not be reproduced or used in any manner whatsoever without the express written permission of the author or publisher except for the use of brief quotations in a book review.

ISBN-13: 978-1-7328798-2-9

ISBN-10: 1-7328798-2-6

 **S-Factor**

What's "S-Factor" you may ask...?

## *S-Factor is Salvation*

Salvation is the most important factor in life, whether we have suffered setbacks or surpassed expectations, severed friendships or strived in relationships, stressed about money or succeeded financially, and struggled with our faith or fully surrendered to God.

We don't earn Salvation. It's a free gift from God that we receive by faith. The evidence, or fruit, of our faith is obedience to God. After accepting His gift, we obey by seeking Jesus daily, standing on God's Word, submitting to the Holy Spirit, and consistently praying[1] through all seasons of life.

– Bridgette Bastien

---

[1] The S-FACTOR PRAYER JOURNAL complements this book and is a great resource to help strengthen your prayer life. It's available at www.prayersavedmylife.com/books.

## *Dedication*

To my brother, BJ,
you're an inspiration to me.

You're a living testimony
that prayer unlocks healing
and God's love does save!

# Table of Contents

Foreword .................................................................. i

Author's Preface ........................................................ v

S-Factor 1: Suicidal .................................................... 1

S-Factor 2: Setbacks and Setups ............................... 17

S-Factor 3: Silent Sufferers ........................................ 33

S-Factor 4: Stolen by Sleep ....................................... 43

S-Factor 5: Sorrow in the Soul .................................. 59

S-Factor 6: Secrets and Schemes .............................. 72

S-Factor 7: Seventy times Seven ............................... 86

S-Factor 8: Speck of Sawdust .................................... 100

S-Factor 9: Seeing the Spirit ...................................... 113

S-Factor 10: Speak, Savior ......................................... 124

S-Factor 11: Seeking Sinners ..................................... 137

S-Factor 12: Sincerely Saved ..................................... 150

S-Factor 13: Salvation in Sychar ................................ 161

S-Factor 14: Simple "?" ............................................... 174

Closing Thoughts: Salvation Is… ................................ 187

Epilogue: A Pastor's Perspective ................................ 195

**Bridgette Bastien**

# *Foreword*

Many years ago, when I worked as a high school Chaplain, we used to take the senior class for a survival week. During the week, the seniors studied about the Great Controversy that our world faces and how God has and is working on our behalf to save humanity. I remember when one of the instructors shared the survival rules of threes—three minutes without air, three hours without shelter in extreme conditions, three days without water, and three weeks without food.

His main purpose of sharing these rules was to point out that most people would die in such extreme conditions—no air, no shelter, no water, no food—without divine intervention. Although, as humans, we boast of our independence and self-sufficiency, we are not as independent as we think we are. We cannot create for ourselves air, materials for a shelter, water, or food out of nothing. All of these essential elements that factor into our existence come from an outside source.

In Genesis chapter one, we read that God spoke and things came into existence just by the sound of His voice. He is the only One that can create something out of nothing. Later on, in the chapter, we read that God creates Adam and Eve in His image and likeness. Due to that image and likeness, we share in God's eternal blessing which brings forth eternal life. The devil, knowing the gift that God has bestowed upon humanity, was angry and devised a plan to bring separation between God and His creation.

How did the devil do it? In Genesis chapter three, we see how men fell for Satan's lies that "We surely would not die." Thinking that they can be like God, Adam and Eve wanted to live a life without the essence of eternity which is God Himself. Sin entered the world due to a choice of disobedience and a sense of self exaltation. It introduces death not only to Adam and Eve, but also to those who come after them. So now as

**Bridgette Bastien**

air, shelter, water and food are vital to our physical life, so a Savior is needed to save us from Death—the wages that sin requires.

Salvation, as air and water, is a factor that can only come from one outside source. The source is Jesus Christ. We are all in need of saving. If that was not so, there would be no reason for God to send His Son to save us from our inherited death sentence. When we acknowledge that truth, it points us to the right path that can only be found in someone not something.

We must also be aware that Satan will always try to discourage us when we begin our journey on the right path. He will bring back ungodly thoughts and may even lead us into circumstances to question God. But as the author, Bridgette Bastien, of this book writes, "Remember that your purpose is greater than your failures." Salvation is much more than a word, an event or an action. It's a promise—

a truth that enables us to raise a banner of liberty because salvation always comes with restoration.

As you journey through S-FACTOR, you'll be able to relate to the stories and see the incredible role that Salvation, along with prayer, plays in the spiritual sanity of our Christian lives. You'll recognize that there is no mythical, unreached or secret path to feel safe and be saved. Salvation is not what we do. It's a state of security, love and compassion given to us by Jesus Christ.

Prayer complements salvation by connecting us to God, allowing us to develop a healthy mental state and an unwavering trust to proclaim, "Though I walk through the valley of the shadow of death, I will fear no evil; For You are with me; Your rod and Your staff, they comfort me" (Psalms 23:4).

**Pastor Jonathan Nino**
*Pastor of Hartford Salem Seventh Day Adventist Church for the Southern New England conference.*

**Bridgette Bastien**

# Author's Preface

If you've read my first book, OVERCOMER, you know that I started on this Prayer Saved My Life (PSML) journey after a near-fatal car accident. At the time, I couldn't have anticipated the voyage God was taking me on or the many lives I would impact by sharing my story. In addition to positively influencing others, I've experienced immense spiritual growth over the past two years, by learning how to surrender fully to God and obeying His voice.

Obedience is the primary reason why this book is entitled S-FACTOR. I wrote most of the book last year but struggled with the title. I relied heavily on God during the writing process. I also prayed often, asking God for guidance in choosing a title. After several months, I had pages of potential titles, but no clear answer from God.

## S-Factor

I was becoming a bit frustrated with His silence and, while attending a women's retreat in Connecticut, I decided to make another request. As I listened to the keynote speaker, I reflected on the intimate stories that God instructed me to share within the PSML series. I decided to have a conversation with Him. Yes, I was debating the Lord in a banquet hall as many people around me were uttering "amen" and "hallelujah."

My conversation with Him went something like this: *God, You've directed me to bare my soul in this book. I've written many chapters, but I'm struggling with the title. How can You be so specific about the book's content, but leave me in the dark regarding the name? What should this book title be, Lord?*

While I was praying, the letter "S" came to my mind. I immediately laughed and shrugged my shoulders, thinking that doesn't make sense. I eventually turned my attention back to the speaker. During her sermon, it seemed as if only words beginning with "s" resonated with me.

Words like *sisters, sorrowful, sanctified, soulful, standup, sincere* and *stepping stone*. I remember laughing out loud and saying, "It's all about 's' today!"

I kept this conversation close to my heart and didn't share it with anyone. I pondered the significance of the letter "s" and contemplated whether anyone would relate to it as a title for the book. Three weeks later while driving with my family, my attention was drawn to the magnificent blue sky, accented by bright sun rays beaming through white fluffy clouds.

Staring at the sky, I saw what I thought was the number "5" carved out of clouds. I hastily took out my phone and snapped several pictures of the sky. While reviewing the images, I soon realized the clouds in the sky formed the letter "S" and not the number "5." I couldn't believe it! Right away, the conversation I had with God several weeks earlier came to mind. I burst into praises. "Thank you, God. You're Awesome," I said. "There is truly no one like You!"

## S-Factor

I saw the letter "S" in the sky as confirmation from God that this book should have an "S" title. I began peppering God with question after question like, "What's significant about 'S'?" and "How does 'S' connect to the *Prayer Saved My Life* series?" I didn't get an answer during that trip but I felt more confident that God was speaking to me and I was eager to obey Him.

The answers to these questions came many weeks later in the wee hours of the morning. While praying, studying, and writing another chapter for the book, it became clear that "S" could stand for anything like spirituality, stewardship, or sin, but I needed to focus on SALVATION. It's all about Salvation!

Once I received this revelation, I felt as if I had been in a dark room and someone turned on the light. I started seeing the common thread between the stories God impressed me to include in this book. They were about salvation.

**Bridgette Bastien**

Indeed, "S-Factor" is all about salvation – being saved from self and sin by God's love.

## S-Factor 1: Suicidal

"Jump!" It was a perfect summer day when I first heard the voice in my head say, "Jump!" I rationalized it as a random, silly thought,

> "The thief does not come except to steal, and to kill, and to destroy. I have come that they may have life, and that they may have it more abundantly."
>
> John 10:10

brushed it off, and then went about my business. However, the other terrifying events of that day made me realize that I was not simply hearing things.

I was not hallucinating, and I was not out of my mind. The suggestion to jump to my death happened not once, but twice in the same day. This was very perplexing because I had much to live for and had made big plans for the future. I silently began wondering if something was wrong

**Bridgette Bastien**

with me. As a child of God, how could suicidal thoughts even enter my mind?

This "S" word, suicide, is a taboo in our society. Still, many people are imprisoned with thoughts of hurting themselves on a daily basis. I became one of those people on a horrific summer day in New York City. Before that day, the thought of hurting myself never entered my mind and the idea of jumping always symbolized happiness.

In fact, children leaping as they play usually put a smile on my face, and a newly engaged woman jumping and screaming, "Yes!" to a lifetime proposal always melts my heart. Life is the most precious gift we have from God. Why would anyone leap off the ground if not but to celebrate life? Where there's life, there's hope, love, and a future.

Jumping is supposed to convey jubilation, but it took on a new meaning for me that day. It became associated with the sinister thought of

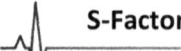 **S-Factor**

suicide. Unfortunately, according to national statistics, I am not alone in this struggle. In 2017, 10.6 million American adults seriously thought about suicide, 3.2 million made a plan, and 1.4 million attempted suicide.[2]

Suicide is now the tenth leading cause of death in America, and it is sweeping through our communities and families. Some people are able to control or ignore suicidal thoughts, while others are trapped by the constant urge to end their lives. It saddens me to admit that I have also experienced the devastating grip of a suicidal spirit.

This spirit tried to snuff me out twice while my family and I explored New York City and rode the Long Island Ferry to Manhattan. The ferry ride started out uneventful as the melting pot of native New Yorkers and tourists from all over the world mixed together. Everyone eagerly

---

[2] Centers for Disease Control and Prevention (CDC) website – Violence Prevention, September 2019.
https://www.cdc.gov/violenceprevention/suicide/fastfact.html

positioned themselves close to the railings on the ferry to admire the sights and spectacular views.

The silhouette of Manhattan's skyline mesmerized us as it glistened with bright, white lights. The reflection of the lights danced on the dark, blue-gray water. The sun settled on the horizon wrapping its magnificent orange and red-glazed shadow around the Statue of Liberty like a well-tailored suit.

Like many of the bright-eyed tourists, I leaned over the ferry railing admiring the breathtaking scenery. The tapestry of nature embracing one of the world's most famous symbols of freedom was unforgettable. Both the sight and the excited expressions on my daughters' faces enthralled me.

Suddenly within my mind, I heard the word, "Jump!" I froze. My mind began racing, and I tried to focus on the rushing water and waves beneath the boat. While captivated by the water's ferociousness, I heard the words again, but more forceful this time, "Jump! Just Jump!"

In my mind, I foresaw my body slipping beneath the rushing water, never to be found again. I envisioned myself fighting vigorously to save my life but losing the fight. This vision frightened me. It stopped my breath. I quickly backed away from the railing. In a daze, I slowly sat down on the bench, while my focus drifted from Lady Liberty to the ferry's floor.

Staring at the floor, I paid attention to the swaying legs of a little boy adjacent to me, the wheels of a baby stroller pivoting back and forth, and the tourists' marching feet—anything to drown out my throbbing heart. Although no one could see that my heart was about to explode, my sweaty palms and shaking knees told the entire fearful story. I was scared out of my mind, but my family had no clue. In that moment, I didn't want to share my despair and spoil our family outing.

**Bridgette Bastien**

After sitting on the bench for a few moments, I realized I heard the same voice earlier in the day. It had an identical terrifying tone and spoke with a distinctive, diabolical sense of suicidal urgency. While shopping and enjoying time with my family at a local mall, this voice tried to persuade me to jump from the second floor.

We were having a wonderful time building bears and picking out the best outfits for them, licking melted ice cream from our hands, and watching the girls chase each other around. During our blissful moment, I decided to lean over the mall's railing to observe the shoppers beneath us who were rushing to and from different stores. This was when I first heard the devilish directive: "Jump!"

I did not utter a word to my girls or husband when I heard it. Instead, I quickly brushed it off and continued enjoying time with my family. Surely, it was only a foolish whim—or at least that is what I thought until later. Hearing the

## S-Factor

suicidal suggestion again and visualizing myself slipping beneath the ferocious water, feelings of confusion, guilt, and shame overwhelmed me.

I did not want to end my life, or did I, at least subconsciously? Was something wrong with me? If so, who should I tell? There were many unanswered questions, and I had no clue what to do. I kept these two incidents in my heart and pondered them for weeks. I prayed almost every day asking God to give me wisdom and discernment.

It appeared that He was not hearing my prayers, until one Sunday afternoon about four weeks after our New York City trip. I was listening to a sermon on television, while cleaning up my bedroom. I heard the pastor say, "When God is ready to take you to another spiritual level, the devil will do everything to stop you. He may even try to take your life. He will try to convince you there is no hope." I stopped in my tracks and stared at the television.

**Bridgette Bastien**

These words were the answer to my prayers and they resonated like music in my ears. I locked my eyes on the pastor, trying to get some visual confirmation that this was indeed a man of God. I did not see any angelic halos or even wings, but the pastor's message was for me. His nicely tailored blue suit with its pinstriped tie quickly lost importance as he expounded on God's will to save His children.

While standing in the middle of my bedroom mesmerized by the pastor's words, God said to me, "The devil wanted you to jump and take your life, but I will make you jump for joy when you overcome and gain the victory." Without thinking, I started jumping up and down in my bedroom—leaping and shouting because God had answered my prayers.

He foretold my victory over my suicidal thoughts and gave me a revelation about that unforgettable day in New York City. These words released me from the guilt, shame, and confusion that shackled me for weeks. They also gave me the courage, several weeks later, to share my story with a church sister, whom we will refer to as "Veronica."

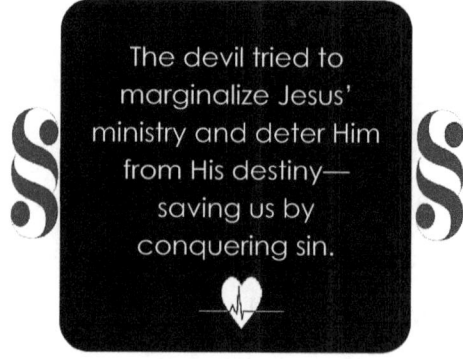

The devil tried to marginalize Jesus' ministry and deter Him from His destiny—saving us by conquering sin.

As I recapped the events at the mall and on the ferry, she exclaimed, "You had the same experience as Jesus!" I laughed out loud and thought with a smile on my face, '*Jesus sailed on many seas, but He was never in a mall.*' Veronica interrupted my thoughts by retelling the story of Jesus' temptation.

She said, "Remember, the devil set Jesus on a pinnacle and said to Him, 'If you are the Son of God, throw yourself down from here'" (Luke 4:9). Satan had the audacity to tell Jesus to jump. He didn't do it to test Christ's faith in God or God's willingness to save His Son. No, the devil tried to marginalize Jesus' ministry and deter Him from His destiny—saving us by conquering sin.

Has Satan been telling you to jump? There should be no shame in admitting it. Are you imprisoned by thoughts of hurting yourself each day? Some people can ignore these thoughts, while others are trapped by suicidal urges. Can you trust someone enough to be honest about your struggles?

Some people have a loving support system with whom they can share such things, while others hold on to their fears in silence. There are many ways to defeat the spiritual foe of suicide, but silence is not the answer. Silence perpetuates a state of hopelessness, triggers depression, and exuberates abusive behaviors. Abusive behavior thrives on silence.

If we remain silent, suicidal thoughts will continue to be an equal opportunity killer. Suicide doesn't care about color, creed, or the community where we live. Wealth and fame are not deterrents either. Consider celebrities such as Kate Spade (fashion designer), Robin Williams (actor and comedian), Anthony Bourdain

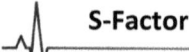 **S-Factor**

(celebrity chef), Marilyn Monroe (actress), Chester Bennington (singer and songwriter), Don Cornelius (television host), Junior Seau (athlete), Jarrid Wilson (pastor), and many more, who have taken their own lives. There are also countless others who have been snatched by this merciless killer, including children, teenagers, and young adults.

Recently, this text came across one of my prayer group chats: "Please pray for Jessica and her son. He made his second suicide attempt in less than a month." My heart sank when I read that message, and I fell to my knees to pray. After praying, I kept on asking, "Why, God?" Sadly, I know deep down that there is not just one answer to that question.

Some people give up hope due to depression, bullying, financial hardship, losing a loved one, and difficult relationships. Regardless of the reason, the rationale written in a suicide note or posted on social media cannot pacify the pain suffered by surviving family members and friends. The trauma of an unsuccessful suicide attempt can last a lifetime.

Only God can heal such a pain. If you're trying to pick up the pieces after losing someone to suicide or trying to prevent a loved one from taking their life, know that there is hope in Christ. There is always hope, no matter what life throws at us. The Bible says, "For I know the thoughts that I think toward you, says the Lord, thoughts of peace and not of evil, to give you a future and a hope" (Jeremiah 29:11).

Any thoughts or spoken words that don't inspire hope isn't of God. It's not God's will that we jump to our deaths or ever experience the pain of losing someone because of suicide. Nor is it God's will that we turn a blind eye to those who are hurting within our sphere of influence. We all have an obligation to remain vigilante and protect those we love.

Like Jessica, we have to stay alert when our family members, friends, neighbors, and colleagues are living in a state of hopelessness and are on the brink of taking their own lives. No one is safe from being pursued by evil or immune to having suicidal thoughts.

God pursues us with love, while the devil persuades us to take our lives. Satan is relentless in achieving his goal to "steal, and to kill and to destroy" (John 10:10, KJV). He uses suicidal thoughts to strangle our aspirations, while shining a light on our failures. He destroys any hope for the future by convincing us there is nothing to live for.

The Bible says, Christ "is also able to save to the uttermost those who come to God through Him, since He always lives to make intercession for them" (Hebrews 7:25). Christ wants to save us and He continually intercedes for us. He makes it possible for us to jump but only in celebration of His love, mercy and grace.

After receiving that text about Jessica, and examining my journey through life and the global impact of suicide, I decided I will never jump. I will not jump off a bannister, a bridge, a ferry, or a freight train—no matter how tough life gets. I'll only leap in anticipation of God's blessings and how He is going to use me to change lives.

I realize it's not always simple for those struggling with suicidal thoughts to just say, "I will not jump," or "I will not take my own life." Such resolutions require supernatural strength from God and unfailing support from someone trustworthy. It also helps to know that, as children of God, our battles may be difficult, but our victory has already been won. All we have to do is believe in Him.

Faith in God will help us counter all suicidal thoughts and withstand the devil's evil persuasion. Satan's intent is that we cast ourselves off the highest pinnacle to deter us from fulfilling our purpose on this earth. God's intent is that we live life to its fullest according to His Word. Knowing this makes all the difference

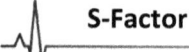 **S-Factor**

when we are at a crossroads between committing suicide and choosing to live.

If you ever have the urge to jump to end your life, remember that your purpose is greater than your failures. If you ever plan to swallow enough pills to fall asleep permanently, remember there is always sunshine and a rainbow after life's storms. If you ever feel pressured to slice your wrists, remember that Christ shed His blood on Calvary so you can have life more abundantly.

If you've already wrote out your suicide letter, I want you to crumple the note or delete it from your computer. Next, I want you to start jumping. Leap towards the ceiling or the sky with confidence. God is willing and able to save you! Levitate off the ground, not to end your life, but to celebrate your past, present and future victories in Christ. Jump! I say, jump!

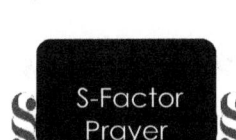

**S-Factor Prayer**

God, suicide is devouring our families. It's taken our kids' lives and pushing us towards the edge. We no longer want to be imprisoned by suicidal thoughts. God, save those who are struggling to make it through each day. Speak to their hearts so they don't give up. If we ever have to encourage someone considering suicide, give us the right words to say at the right time. We want to be a source of strength for those who are weak. Give us hope in this world of death and despair. Save us, Lord!

# S-Factor 2: Setbacks and Setups

I was on the brink of death. Seriously, I was holding onto the car door for dear life. The store fronts

> "And we know that all things work together for good to those who love God, to those who are the called according to His purpose."
>
> Romans 8:28

and billboards vanished within a blink of an eye as we sped down Crenshaw Boulevard in Los Angeles, California, at twice the speed limit.

Sometimes, we barely beat the stop lights and other times slamming on the brakes was our only saving grace. I lost count of how many times my body lifted from the front seat and came crashing down because of how quickly we sped over potholes and speed bumps. Gripping the door handle was the only way to prevent my body from swaying from side to side or hitting the dashboard.

The driver was also being tossed around, but she seemed unaffected by the physical discomfort of the ride. This was not an episode of a couple of teenagers out joy-riding at 1a.m. in the morning. Instead, this was a volcanic explosion of pain, hurt, and anger that had been trapped beneath a mother's heart for several months.

I cannot explain why her breakdown happened at that moment. I can only assume that her heart could no longer contain the ache of a mother seeing her son suffering daily and it erupted in anguish. She released a cry filled with shrills and bellows which went through my bones and crushed my spirit. I can still feel the rhythm – BOOM, BOOM, BOOM – as my mother pounded the steering wheel and cried sorrowfully. There were many words said during that ride, but the repetition of "Why? Why? Why?" still resounds in my memory.

My mother and I were coming home from Cedar Sinai Hospital after another long day and

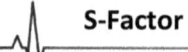 S-Factor

several months of caring for my baby brother, BJ. He was in the Intensive Care Unit and things grew dim as the days went by. Throughout my mom's pregnancy, BJ was healthy and strong. He was a big baby but there were no pre-birth complications. The day of his birth should've been one of rejoicing. However, it was the start of years filled with tears, pain, unanswered questions, and moments of doubting God's love. It was our family's setback!

Several of BJ's nerves were ripped out of his spine during birth. The doctor used a medical vacuum to extract him from the womb causing irreversible damage leading to Brachial Plexus Palsy (BPP). BPP is a disorder that limits a person's ability to move and maintain balance and posture. BPP was also the beginning of my family's trials and tribulations.

This injury left BJ's right arm paralyzed, his diaphragm needing plication (surgically flattening it to give his lung more space to expand), and many other medical complications. The medical severity of his injury was too much to comprehend at times, but the impact was obvious to all. It forever changed the trajectory of my family's future plans.

Over the past two decades, BJ has had countless hospital visits, numerous surgeries, and ongoing doctor visits and therapy sessions. After some time, I became sick of the brightness of sterile white coats and the disinfectant smell in the hospital rooms. And when people would stare at BJ's paralyzed arm, I found myself becoming frustrated and angry.

We were physically and emotionally exhausted from arriving at the hospital by 6:30 a.m. each morning and leaving well after midnight. My mom and I became permanent fixtures at the hospital, but it never felt like home. I remember feeling helpless each morning when we arrived at the hospital and hopeless as we left my brother in the Intensive Care Unit each night.

## S-Factor

At this time, I was in my early twenties and all I could do for my brother was pray that God would take away his pain, heal his body, and save his life. I prayed often and earnestly during this season of our lives. The experience not only left BJ physically broken, but our family emotionally shattered as well.

It was difficult to deal with setbacks wrapped in medical malpractice, depleting finances, and a life-changing disability. It was difficult not to be emotionally broken when there were so many unanswered questions. Why did this happen to our family? What could we have done differently? Will tomorrow be better, or should we just give up hope? Will our family ever be the same?

Everyone goes through challenging times in life, but there are some situations that leave lasting imprints on our minds, bodies and souls. BJ's injury at birth was one of those life-changing incidents. My family oscillated between moments of sorrow and happiness, as well as bitterness and sweetness.

Sorrow came from the disappointment of wanting to be home with our new bundle of joy instead of living in the hospital for several months. Bitterness came from being on an emotional, legal, and medical roller coaster that many families with sick members are forced to ride. Worst of all was witnessing the suffering of an innocent child without the power to stop it.

Despite the dark moments and seasons of gloom, there were also gleams of light. Light came from the sweetness and love shown by many strangers. BJ's heartbeat and smile expressed happiness whenever my mother held him in her arms. He was connected to countless machines in the Intensive Care Unit, but the joy radiating from him deafened the beeping sounds.

When my family thought we couldn't make it another day, prayer and faith in God's

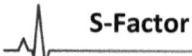 S-Factor

Word made the difference between total despair and hope. We lived by the scripture, "And it shall come to pass that whoever calls on the name of the Lord shall be saved" (Acts 2:21). Without fail, we called on Jesus daily and saw the manifestation of His power and salvation.

Again, and again, BJ reached developmental milestones that many doctors and medical specialists doubted he would ever attain. Our faith was strengthened each time medical experts said, "No," but God said, "Yes." After each setback, there was always a miraculous setup. His journey from birth to now has defied all odds. We believe he is a living testimony of God's promises and saving grace, not just a product of medical breakthroughs.

As I reflect on BJ's journey, the Bible story of Mephibosheth comes to mind. He was the grandson of King Saul and son of Jonathan. After his father's death and his grandfather's suicide, Mephibosheth became crippled in the feet. At the age of five, his nurse dropped him while attempting to flee and save his life (2 Samuel 4:4). I can imagine how his physical brokenness made his life difficult.

His nobility couldn't even soften the fall or strengthen his lame feet. This was his setback. He lived in a desolate place, Lo Debar, and probably lost hope after years of having to depend on others for his basic needs. I am sure Mephibosheth was in despair, but God had a divine plan in place. It began with a special invitation from the reigning king.

King David summoning Mephibosheth to the palace must have been a frightening experience for him. After all, why would the reigning king want a cripple in the royal palace, or even in his presence? Mephibosheth was no doubt dumbfounded when "David said unto him, 'Fear not: for I will surely shew thee kindness for Jonathan thy father's sake, and will restore thee all the land of Saul thy father; and thou shalt eat bread at my table continually'" (2 Samuel 9:7, KJV).

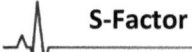 S-Factor

His countenance must have changed when he realized he wouldn't be punished or killed. God worked through David to restore Mephibosheth to royalty. His life would be spared; he would have the king's protection and a place at the king's table forever. His salvation was secured by God and salvation always comes with restoration.

Restoration is also a wonderful gift from our Heavenly Father. I was reminded of this during a Mary Grace Gellekanao concert. Mary Grace is a pianist, but she is not like other musicians. Her setback began while she was in her mother's womb. Mary was born without her right forearm and with an undersized leg.

Like BJ, her congenital disability made her early life very difficult, but that didn't deter her destiny. Despite her heart-breaking beginning, she is now an internationally acclaimed pianist who performs in world-renowned concert halls like the John F. Kennedy Center for the Performing Arts in Washington, D.C.

**Bridgette Bastien**

During the concert, Mary Grace captivated us all with every stroke of the piano keys. As she played, her right arm, which ends in a stump right below the elbow, masterfully hit one key at a time while her left arm led the way in creating beautiful music that penetrated the soul.

Her talent and artistry spoke volumes about how our brokenness can be beautifully mended through Christ. God used her setback to set her up for greatness and to inspire others. By sharing her story and talent with us, Mary Grace led us through an emotional metamorphosis from sorrow and pity to jubilation and praise.

Mephibosheth and Mary Grace both went from being broken to being divinely blessed by God. Their stories should remind us that our brokenness, whether it happened before birth (Mary Grace), during birth (BJ), or after birth (Mephibosheth), is not a prediction of our destiny. No matter how devastating our

**S-Factor**

setbacks, God's saving grace prepares us for divine setups.

BJ, at twenty-two years old, is now learning this lesson and

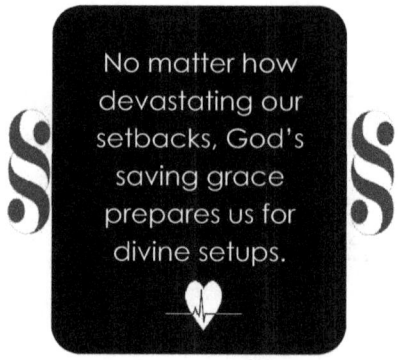

> No matter how devastating our setbacks, God's saving grace prepares us for divine setups.

beginning to view himself not through the eyes of others but through God's eyes. A few weeks ago, when we spoke about his life's journey, BJ said:

> *Prayer has led me to God. I draw closer to Him through scriptures and learning from stories of people in the Bible. Even though I may not fully understand why He allowed me to be injured during birth or why my arm is paralyzed, I believe He saved my life and has a specific job for me to do in my lifetime.*
> 
> *Sometimes, I can barely lift my arm to do daily activities (i.e. tying my shoelaces, buttoning my pants or shirts,*

**Bridgette Bastien**

*taking a bath, and trying to clean my left arm or the left side of my back), however, I cannot complain because, overall, my life has been a nice one. I don't want to use the words "easy" or "hard" because everyone's life can be easy and hard at different times.*

*My life has been good because of a supportive family. The people I often interact with are usually very caring. I can only remember once or twice when I was bullied because of my disability. My reaction then was to just shrug it off and ignore those mean people because I have supportive loved ones.*

*From a young age, my family has always encouraged me to be all that I can be, even when I doubted my abilities. Last year, I participated in a commercial for a gaming program*

### S-Factor

called Copilot. It helps kids with disabilities learn to play video games.

During the screening interview, I showed the directors and producers how I play various games. They were very impressed with my skill level because my right arm has been paralyzed from birth. I was also surprised that no one in the group played as well as I did. This experience made me realize that I had accomplished things that even kids with two functioning arms have struggled to do.

I am slowly finding myself and setting goals for the things I want to accomplish. I know that God loves all His children, no matter if they are disabled, orphans, or just in a rough situation. To those who are disabled, I would say, it's OK to feel down sometimes. The most important thing is to never give up. We may fall more *often than others, but by relying on God, we will always have the strength to get back up again.*

*All we need to do is have faith in God and believe that we can be successful. I may be reaching my goals slower than my peers, but in ten years, I see myself as a college graduate with a successful career in quality testing video games. My disability doesn't have to define who I am.*

*I believe in myself and fully agree with this quote: "Life always offers you a second chance—it's called tomorrow."[3] Tomorrow offers hope to those disabled and enabled. NEVER GIVE UP!*

I cannot claim to know the future, but I agree with my brother. God saved his life for a purpose. Like BJ, some of us are marred or

---

[3] Quote by Dylan Thomas

## S-Factor

broken, either spiritually, emotionally, or physically. Like my mother, we face challenges that we smile through for some time, until that one day comes when we can no longer smile.

The floodgates will eventually open, spilling out months or even years, of suppressed frustration and tears. It's hard to contain anything in broken vessels. However, in the hands of God, the Potter, our broken and missing pieces can be put back together into vessels that reflect His honor and glory.

We strive daily to reflect Christ and over the years, my family has learned many lessons. We now know that brokenness is not meant to destroy, but to demonstrate the power of God (John 9:2, 3). We understand the importance of embracing our setbacks because they prepare us for divine setups. If you are facing similar challenges in life, join us in prayerfully awaiting restoration and completeness in Christ.

**Bridgette Bastien**

*Your Word says that You are the Potter and we are the clay. Lord, continue to make and mold us into what You want us to be. We tend to focus on our broken parts and lament over how unfair life can be. Help us to learn that brokenness is not an eternal curse and that our setbacks are not reasons to despair. Continue to remind us that You have already done all You can to save us and set us up for greatness. Remind us to uplift others as they strive to live out their purpose amidst setbacks. Even during our tough seasons, may we live in such a way that mockers and doubters will have to confess that You are the true and living God.*

## S-Factor 3: Silent Sufferers

I didn't fully understand why my mom's cries were filled with shrills and bellows when my brother was in the hospital, but I get it

> "He was oppressed and He was afflicted, Yet He opened not His mouth."
>
> Isaiah 53:7

now. She was a silent sufferer who could no longer remain quiet. After many months of suppressing her emotions, she had to let them out. I often reflect on that traumatic car ride whenever I find myself screaming inside. Right now, I'm hollering from the depths of my soul as these words are being etched in paper. Can you relate to such internal turmoil?

While some folks will shout their problems from the rooftops or post them on social media, others prefer to remain speechless. I've always been the silent type so I'd rather yell on the inside. My internal scream is so loud that if I did

**Bridgette Bastien**

open my mouth, the earth would shake and be thrown off its axis. Sadly, I just can't find the strength to unlock my lips.

The pain is not physical and it's undetectable to those around me. It runs deeper than the natural eye can see. I want to share this anguish, and I need to let it out, but who will care? My spirit is crushed and my voice is suppressed, yet no one takes the time to ask or tries to understand my silence. I am not angry about dealing with my anguish alone because most people are dealing with their own issues.

Are you suffering in silence? Suffering is part of life's journey in this sinful world, but suffering silently destroys us from the inside out. If you're bottling up your fears, afflictions, and failures, you no longer have to, there's hope. Christ knows what it means to suffer in silence. Isaiah 53:7 says, "He was oppressed and He was afflicted, yet He opened not His mouth; He was led as a lamb to the slaughter, and as a sheep before its shearers is silent, so He opened not His mouth."

## S-Factor

We are most like Christ when we remain silent while under attack. During His arrest, trial, and crucifixion, Jesus was either completely silent or said only a few words. I believe He refrained from speaking because He knew the power of His words. He would've destroyed the universe by simply opening His mouth. Unlike Jesus, many of us suffer in silence, not to contain our strength, but because we feel powerless.

Jesus had unimaginable power because He stayed connected to God. This enabled Him to carry His cross despite the torment and lay down His life at Calvary. Jesus' sacrifice was the only way we could've been saved from sin. Although Jesus voluntarily picked up His cross, we often have crosses laid upon us. Situations like being trapped in dead-end relationships or jobs, dealing with death or divorce, struggling through chronic illness or the current pandemic—all of these heavy burdens drive us to stifle our cries.

Unfortunately, suffering in silence is nothing new. It's just as prevalent today as it was in biblical times. Hagar's story in Genesis 16 and 21 is a perfect example of how a stressful life can turn into internal turmoil. Let's remove our sneakers (or stilettoes) and step into Hagar's sandals. Hagar was an Egyptian slave belonging to Sarai, Abram's wife. Sarai was dealing with her own issues of infertility and offered Hagar to Abram so he could have an heir. What if you were forced to sleep with someone's spouse to benefit their marriage?

Abram slept with Hagar and as soon as she got pregnant, conflict arose between her and Sarai (Genesis 16:4-6). Most Christians usually focus on Abram and Sarai's side of the story, but can you imagine what Hagar was going through during this time? She didn't ask to be a slave, request to sleep with Abram, or want to bare his child. Those decisions were made for her. She had no say in the trajectory of her life or how her body was being used by others.

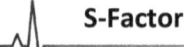 S-Factor

Hagar became a silent sufferer as a pregnant, enslaved foreigner with no status or rights. Life became so unbearable that Hagar decided to run away. Are you contemplating running away because of your circumstances? Don't lose faith. God will make a way out of no way.

> Slaves are not saved or granted freedom simply because they are industrious and bear fruit.

Before we focus on how God stepped in to save Hagar, it's noteworthy that Hagar remained a silent sufferer even after her son, Ishmael, was born. I'm sure she assumed that things would get better once she gave Abram an heir. Many times, we are screaming inside, while also believing that once we reach a certain milestone, life will be better. Hagar had to learn the hard way. Slaves are not saved or granted freedom simply because they are industrious and bear fruit. Hagar couldn't free herself and neither

**Bridgette Bastien**

can anyone who is suffering today in silence. Salvation is possible only through Jesus.

God saved Hagar's life twice. The first time was in Genesis 16 when an angel of the Lord found her in the desert, urged her to return to Abram, and promised that her unborn child would become a great nation. Hagar believed the Lord and "Called the name of the Lord who spoke to her, 'You-Are-the-God-Who-Sees,' for she said, 'Have I also here seen Him who sees me?'" (Genesis 16:13) She was running away with no plan or resources. We can't escape our present dilemmas without a divinely sanctioned plan for the future. God intervened to let Hagar know that her suffering was not in vain. The Lord made it clear that He saw her afflictions.

What is love, if not to be seen? Many people scream in silence because they are invisible to others. In your current situation, are you wondering if God sees you? He not only sees everything, but He also hears the bellows from deep within our souls. Hagar must have been

## S-Factor

relieved to have someone acknowledge her suffering. Her response, "You Are the God Who Sees Me" is incredibly profound. Hagar thought that no one cared to notice her suffering; but the Lord had seen, the Lord had heard.

The second time God saved Hagar's life was in Genesis 21. She didn't run away this time, instead she was banished by Abram because of Sarai. With only "bread and a skin of water" (verse 14), Hagar and young Ishmael were exiled into the Wilderness of Beersheba to fend for themselves. Our wilderness experiences can be brutal—food scarcity, isolation, and danger all around. Yet I've found that during these rough seasons, I'm more receptive to God's voice and the manifestation of His power.

Like most of us would, Hagar lost hope when she ran out of bread and water. She prepared for death, but God showed up. The Bible says, "God opened her eyes, and she saw a well of water. And she went and filled the skin with water, and gave the lad a drink" (Genesis

21:19). Many times, when we feel completely helpless, we tend to close our eyes and yell. While our eyes are shut and we are screaming, we cannot see or hear anything, not even God. It's during these times that the Lord has to open our eyes to behold the full picture—a well of water to quench our immediate thirst and a promise of becoming a great nation in the future.

I've learned to fast and earnestly pray whenever I am suffering in silence and screaming internally. I understand that it doesn't really matter why I am screaming at that moment because life will always give us something to yell about. I also don't eagerly share my sorrows with others. Some folks, even with best of intentions, can't handle the weight of our woes. The comfort they can provide is often inadequate. Their advice may even be detrimental to our healing and growth. Bottomline, God is the best advisor during our seasons of internal turmoil.

I've never been led astray after prayerfully seeking God's guidance and crying out to Him for help. I often pray for God to open my eyes, to calm the storm within me, and for a cup of His "living water" (John 4:10) which quenches every thirst. He always answer this prayer. My situation may not change right away, but I get divine perspective and peace in the moment. At which point, I usually proclaim, "You are the God who sees me" because only those who truly care about us, can see and hear us even when we're quiet.

If you are suffering in silence, God sees you. He gave Jesus the power He needed to die on Calvary's cross. He saved Hagar not once, but twice. God knows our struggles and He has already prophesied that they'll not break us, but instead, will build us up for His honor and glory. Once we turn everything over to God, He will do what only He can do. He will transform our silent screams into shouts of praises. With such a promise, we don't have to suffer in silence because of our struggles and setbacks. We just have to surrender to the Lord.

**Bridgette Bastien**

*Jesus, I need to surrender all to You. I love being in control, but when things fall apart, I sometimes crumble. I'm not alone. Many people prefer to remain speechless while bottling up their fears and failures. Help us, Lord. Silence is not always the best solution. Give us the strength to share our struggles without jeopardizing Your plans for us. God save your children who suffer in silence. I'm asking that You rescue and restore us so our voices can be heard especially in challenging times.*

# S-Factor 4: Stolen by Sleep

"Hello? Hello. Yes, she's right here. Wake up baby, wake up." Wrapped in a sense urgency, these words woke me out of my slumber. As my

> "Jesus said to her, 'I am the resurrection and the life. He who believes in Me, though he may die, he shall live.'"
>
> John 11:25

husband, Paul, handed me the phone, I could hear the voice of my brother, Wayne.

I was in a daze and couldn't quite understand what he was trying to say to me. Eventually, the words "he died" registered in my ears, and I quickly sat up in bed. I didn't know if I was to scream, cry, or remain silent. All I knew was that on Sunday, March 18th while I slept, our father, Craig, took his last breath.

My father's death became a reality before I said my last goodbye. I yearned to hear his voice again and to see his face one more time. If

**Bridgette Bastien**

I could've turn back the hand of time, I wouldn't have fallen asleep the night before he died. I would've done everything in my power to stay awake and spend those last moments with my father. It's ironic because I went decades without seeing or speaking to him, but when terminal cancer became our family's fight, God used it to repair relationships, reunite siblings, and ultimately, save our father.

Before our father became ill, I never thought reconciliation was possible. I prayed about our relationship for many years, but those prayers were often filled with resentment and anger. I even grappled with obeying God's word, "Honor your father and mother, which is the first commandment with promise" (Ephesians 6:2, NKJV) and opening myself up for emotional pain. I was infected by so much fury that after learning he had cancer, I refused to visit him.

Every child wants to have a strong and loving relationship with their biological parents. When that relationship is non-existent, or it has

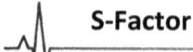

## S-Factor

been severed, abandonment will grow into resentment. My bitterness towards my father for being absent most of my life manifested into a desire for revenge. I wanted him to know what it felt like to be cast aside when you needed support.

I was saddened by the news but hesitated to drop everything and make the long journey to Canada. My brothers, Wayne and Kevin, eventually convinced me to make the trip. Several weeks later, I was on a plane heading to Saskatchewan. The importance of that visit didn't hit me until I sat in the Toronto Pearson International Airport awaiting my connecting flight. As I watched bustling tourists struggling with their luggage, exhausted children whining and escaping their parents' grip, as well as tired workers faking smiles at each new customer ordering food, I began imagining what our reunion would be like.

For over two decades, I dramatized the reunion with my father in my head. I memorized all the things I would say to him, such as expressing my disappointment that he was an absentee father and vocalizing how unfair it was for children to suffer because of their parents' selfishness. I had it all planned out, but my plans did not come to fruition when I actually saw him face to face.

    Kevin and I walked through our father's front door not knowing what to expect based on the cancer's progression. In my mind, I still envisioned him as the strong vivacious man I knew as a young girl. However, my memories were very different from reality. His frail body softened my hardened heart. My childhood hurt was still present, but I didn't have the desire to crush his spirit when I saw the excitement in his eyes.

    I can still remember his eyes full of joy as Kevin and I entered his home. The funny and vibrant man we once knew was still there, but it was entirely evident that cancer was taking its toll. His frame was smaller and his face was

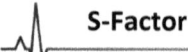 **S-Factor**

sunken in, but his energy was like fireworks on the 4th of July, and his eyes were full of vitality. After settling in and going through the niceties, I decided to get down to business. Yes, I was on a mission. I planned to pack decades of missed opportunities into four days.

I started asking tons of questions. I probed him with questions to extract as much information as possible—about our family history, his early days, and why he made certain decisions in life. As we sprinted down memory lane, I felt my childhood fury fading away and the emptiness being filled by empathy. I began to realize that he was a fallible human. He made decisions based on his pursuit of happiness and his family's expectations. I listened to story after story with a desire to inhale every moment of his past.

His stories were both admirable and appalling to me. I realized that my father was an overachiever in school who took pleasure in acing his exams—we had that much in common. I remember bawling for days whenever I received any grades lower than an "A" in school. I perked up as he shared details of his electrical technician job in Jamaica.

As a former chemist, I'm always intrigued by science and math. He gave Kevin and me a glimpse into the "old days" and the world of repairing and restoring television sets, radios, refrigerators, stereos, and other home electronics systems. You know, the times before social media, iPhones, texting, and unlimited television channels.

I saw myself in him on a professional level. But on a personal level, we were like night and day. His stories about being a "ladies' man" didn't sit well with me. I expressed my annoyance during some of his lavish playboy stories, but I didn't have the power to turn back time. As we continued down memory lane, I begrudgingly thought about how one single decision can have lifetime consequences. We often make selfish decisions without fully understanding the impact those decisions could have. Just after that

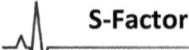 **S-Factor**

thought crossed my mind, my father's wife entered the room, bursting with joy.

Mrs. Craig happily announced that she had spoken to their pastor and his baptism was confirmed for the following day. Then, as quickly as she entered the room, she left. I turned my attention back to my father, who was smiling from ear to ear. Suddenly, my thought about 'one single decision having lifetime consequences' no longer had a negative connotation. His decision to accept the free gift of salvation and be baptized was the most important decision he could ever make. My heart melted and I finally understood why God had me take the trip to Canada.

The Bible says, "The Lord is righteous in all His ways, gracious in all His works" (Psalms 145:17). I can confirm this is true by the way God worked in my father's life. Like many people, my father resisted surrendering his heart to Christ for years, but God continued to pursue him. The consistent prayer of family members and friends made the ultimate difference.

> God is eager to save each of us, regardless of our past.

While sitting at his bedside and watching him smile, I was reminded that the gift of salvation is available to everyone. It's never too late to accept it, once we're alive. I also smiled thinking about the scripture that says, "He that believeth and is baptized shall be saved; but he that believeth not shall be damned" (Mark 16:16, KJV). God is eager to save each of us, regardless of our past. My father was a living testimony. All we have to do is open our hearts to God's unfailing love.

As I was pondering God's unconditional love, my father urgently called my name, touched my forearm, and grabbed my attention. I could tell by the worried look in his eyes that he was eager to get something off his chest. He stared at me for a while before whispering, "you asked me earlier, what's my greatest fear? My

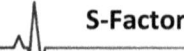 **S-Factor**

fear is that my children..." He abruptly stopped talking in the middle of his sentence and began wiping his eyes. As tears ran down his face onto his blue and white striped pajamas, I sat next to him in silence. I didn't know what to say or do.

I couldn't recall asking him about his greatest fear, but obviously it was something he had contemplated for years. The silence lasted for several minutes and served as a buffer to give him the courage he needed to continue our conversation. He finally broke the silence by saying: "I spoke to all my kids over the years because they called me, except for you. Why didn't you ever call me? What do you really think of me?"

These questions caught me off guard, because my plan was to be the interrogator, not the interrogated. Unable to find my voice, I gestured with my hands, making roller coaster motions as I attempted to demonstrate the emotional ups and downs of our relationship. It was the only thing I could think of doing while garnering enough courage to be blatantly and unapologetically honest.

When I finally began speaking, my heart expressed these words, "I loved you when I was a young girl, but I resented you as a teenager. Now as an adult, I've decided to put all that emotional baggage behind me and I can honestly say that you are OK in my book." I stopped talking after uttering these words because I could see that they had hit a target.

My father adjusted his body on the bed to sit up until we were almost face to face. "I was hoping that when you got older you would understand," he said in a solemn tone. I was about to tell him that I really didn't understand how a father could abandon his child, but before I could say another word, he slumped back down onto the bed, covered his face with a pair of blue pants lying next to him, and wept.

I listened to his muffled sobs and watched the tears stream down his neck. Looking at him, I

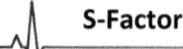
S-Factor

thought about how parents are often seen as giants in their children's eyes and are usually providers, counselors, and protectors. In that moment, however, I saw none of these things. Instead, I saw a feeble man with a strong spirit trying to make the best of his current situation. He was no longer able to protect or provide for his children, now he needed support and reassurance.

He eventually removed the pants from his face, wiped his eyes and quickly changed the topic from our estranged relationship to Canada's weather. Although he changed topics, the sadness in the room lingered. It was like a thick fog that permeated the air during each rainy and cold winter season. We both engaged in the weather discussion like expert meteorologists. However deep down, we knew that there was no topic of conversation that could erase all those years of pain.

Unfortunately, we had missed out on many memorable moments. We could've talked nonstop for months and still not re-capture those moments. We did our best to live in the present and maximize the time that we had together. Despite his health conditions, our days were filled mostly with joy and laughter. I left Canada with a renewed desire to strengthen our relationship by communicating more often.

Unfortunately, within six months of visiting, he died. The sleep of death stole his life away and left our hearts shattered in pieces. It snatched him from his family and friends; it crushed our hopes of hearing more of his captivating stories. We knew death was inevitable, but we did not know the day or hour it would happen.

On the day my father died, these words permeated my mind: "Therefore let us not sleep, as do others; but let us watch and be sober. For they that sleep, sleep in the night; and they that be drunken are drunken in the night. But let us, who are of the day, be sober, putting on the breastplate of faith and love; and for an helmet, the hope of salvation" (1 Thessalonians 5:6-8,

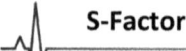 **S-Factor**

KJV). Ironically, the Holy Spirit led me to read that entire chapter a week before the dreadful day. I read it many times, but didn't fully understand the message or implications. By the time I understood the message, it was too late.

The day before he died, I watched my father on Skype—he was laying unresponsive in bed. I promised his wife I would call again when I returned home the following day. After driving several hours home and preparing for the week ahead, I was exhausted. Instead of calling, I texted, "Good night, I'll give him a call tomorrow." His wife responded, "OK. Have a good night. Talk tomorrow." I never got the chance to follow through on that promise because my dad died that night. I will never be able to speak with him again. For my dad and me, tomorrow will never come.

In the days following his death, I wrestled with not being able to say goodbye. The farewell to my father was not what I envisioned during his months of illness. I wanted to be by his bedside or

**Bridgette Bastien**

at least watch him on video taking his last breath. Instead, I was forced to say farewell to a room full of people, some of whom I did not know. This experience was sad because I felt alone despite being surrounded by many people. Sleep stole our father away and left me with nothing but a few memories and a heart full of sorrow.

Since his death, I've reflected on the imminent return of Jesus Christ. I knew my dad would inevitably pass away because of his illness, but I didn't believe it would happen that quickly. Likewise, many of us have heard for years that Jesus is coming back, but we remain spiritually asleep, not believing He will come again very soon. We have become too busy, too tired, or too sleepy to prepare for His return. Some even delay surrendering their lives to God thinking that tomorrow is promised to them.

Matthew 24:36, 37 (KJV) reminds us, "But of that day and hour knoweth no man, no, not the angels of heaven, but my Father only. But as the days of Noah were, so shall also the coming of

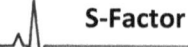 S-Factor

the Son of Man be." We must stay awake, and like the five wise virgins, have extra oil in our lamps while we wait for the bridegroom. Do you have extra oil?

We don't want Christ to return if we aren't prepared to meet Him. We also don't want the sleep of death to steal us away from our loved ones before we get the chance to accept God's free gift of salvation. Just like I couldn't regain those years without my father, we won't be able to turn back time if we've missed out on having a relationship with our heavenly Father. Let's seek Him now while we can.

 *Thank You, God, for allowing us to mend our broken relationships. In our hustle and bustle, we often forget that life is short. Often, because of hurt and pride, we don't try to reconcile. We mistakenly think we have tomorrow to make things right. Tomorrow is not promised to anyone. Continue to divinely knock down the walls we have built around our hearts. I*

**Bridgette Bastien**

*am grateful that You touched my father's heart and saved his soul before sleep stole him away. Saying goodbye is always difficult, but Your love continues to pursue us. You comfort us by wrapping us in Your merciful arms. Keep us in Your arms forever.*

## S-Factor 5: Sorrow in the Soul

Death is a worthy adversary that only God has the power to defeat. It respects no one and pursues its prey with a forceful intensity. I was

> *"The Lord is near to the brokenhearted and saves those who are crushed in spirit."*
>
> Psalms 34:18

reminded of death's unbiased pursuit of innocent lives not too long ago. I was doing house work while fussing about my girls not cleaning up their messes when my cell phone started buzzing rhythmically. As I picked up the phone, the caller exclaimed, "You have to get to the hospital now. She lost the baby."

My heart dropped immediately and I threw down the dust rag and furniture polish. I hastily washed my hands, put on a pair of clean jeans and a casual blazer, grabbed my purse and keys then rushed out the door. I didn't slow down until

**Bridgette Bastien**

I was outside the specified hospital room. I paused for a moment and took a deep breath.

As I slowly walked into the pale-yellow room, I sensed a feeling of emptiness. I said hello to everyone and quickly directed my focus toward the bewildered mother. My church sister, whom we will refer to as "Janet," was laying on the hospital bed in a baby-blue hospital gown with tubes everywhere and multiple machines pulsing their own tune. The light buzzing overhead battled for my attention, but her eyes pulled me in like a vacuum.

I sat next to Janet and held her hands. Without me asking, she began re-telling the story of how she had lost her baby. Can you imagine carrying a baby for nine months, receiving good medical reviews during your doctor's visits, then suddenly learning, two days before the due date, that they cannot detect a heartbeat? Janet stopped talking and, except for the rhythmic sounds of the machines and the buzzing lights, the room was silent.

## S-Factor

To break the silence, I rose from the chair and walked over to the expectant father. After giving him a hug of condolence, I returned to Janet. We all sat quietly because no words could express the loss. It's amazing how many things you notice with your eyes when surrounded by silence. Things like the nervous twitches of a despondent aunt, the perplexed stare of a grieving father, and the upright posture of a caring pastor.

After about 15 mins, Janet cried out, "Why? Why?" with a groan and look of uncertainty in her eyes. Answering her own question with tears quietly flowing from her eyes, she said, "I don't know why, but I am trusting you, Lord." Her tears ran down her dark brown cheeks and neck only to settle in a pool of misery on her hospital gown.

If those tears could talk, I'm sure they would scream, "Lord take this pain and heartache away." I squeezed her hands to offer some reassurance, but that caused the intensity of her tears to increase more. I began to silently pray that God would remove the sorrow from her soul.

I prayed, "God, I'm not going to ask You why, because even if You gave an answer, I wouldn't understand it. My request is that You grant my sister peace. Wrap Your arms tight around this family so that they feel Your presence every moment of every day." As I prayed, Janet's tears stopped flowing and she stared at the wall in silence. I hesitantly touched her swollen belly where the baby still resided. I silently cried out, "God, if it's Your will, I know You can bring this child back to life. Let Your will be done. Please Lord!"

Accepting God's will when it brings heartache requires the Holy Spirit. I needed the Spirit to grant me fortitude in that moment. After my prayer, I sat back in the chair with an empty feeling. I couldn't help reflecting on giving birth and the sting of death. The birth of a child is usually a joyous occasion. It erases the memory

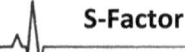 S-Factor

of birth pains for most mothers and knits family members together like a tapestry. It puts smiles on the faces of complete strangers and renders applause from nurses and doctors. Birth is often celebrated because it symbolizes hope and a brighter future.

Unlike birth, death evokes a very different set of emotions and reactions. Anyone who has lost a child or a loved one knows this painful fact. Death causes sorrow in the soul and leaves people feeling empty, broken, terrified, and sad. Often times, those who mourn cannot find the words to express the emotional turmoil they are going through. Many mourners long for death themselves because the pain is just too much to bear. I can imagine how the agony is intensified when it's a baby that's stolen by sleep.

The anguish of losing a child is exemplified in a few touching biblical stories. One of my favorites can be found in 1 Kings 3:16-28. Two harlots (prostitutes) came to Solomon, the ruling king, to resolve a dilemma between them. They

**Bridgette Bastien**

lived in the same house and each gave birth to a son within three days of each other. One woman's son died during the night. Under the cover of darkness, while the other mother slept, she switched her dead infant with the living baby. When the real mother arose in the morning, she realized that the child in her arms was not only dead, but it wasn't her baby!

Obviously, a conflict arose between the women and both claimed to be the living child's mother. They brought the case before King Solomon to judge it. Solomon, the wisest man who ever lived, decided to test the mothers' love for the child. He asked for a sword and said, "Divide the living child in two, and give half to the one, and half to the other" (1 Kings 3:25, KJV). What would you have done in that situation? The real mother's stomach must have churned, and sorrow stirred in her soul as she thought about her baby being killed.

She responded, "O my lord, give her the living child, and in no wise slay it." But the other,

**S-Factor**

deceitful mother said, "Let it be neither mine nor thine, but divide it" (verse 26). The real mother's boldness and display of undeniable love

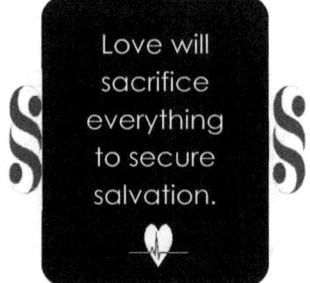
Love will sacrifice everything to secure salvation.

made an impression on Solomon. He wisely discerned that only the child's mother would rather give him up than witness his death. The king answered and said, "Give her, [the real mother], the living child, and in no wise slay it" (verse 28).

God saved that baby boy's life by giving Solomon divine insight and revealing that love knows no bounds. The Bible says that, "Love never fails" 1 Corinthians 13:8. Love will sacrifice everything to secure salvation. This was evident in the harlot's story. Without a doubt, most mothers would give everything, and do anything, to spare their child's life. Most fathers, just like mothers, feel pain when their children suffer and will withhold nothing to ease the suffering.

This is exemplified by the story in Mark 5:22-43. Jairus, a church leader, did all he could to save his child. He humbly went to Jesus and begged Him to save his twelve-year-old daughter (verse 23). Jesus eagerly decided to go to Jairus' house. On the way there, Jesus stopped in the midst of the journey to minister to a woman in need. While he impatiently waited on Jesus, Jairus' servant approached them and said, "Thy daughter is dead: why troublest thou the Master any further?" (Mark 5:35, KJV)

I can't imagine the sorrow in Jairus' soul when he heard those words. The news of his daughter's passing must have rocked him to the core. His worst nightmare became a reality as death made its appearance. Jairus probably lost his composure and was on the cusp of a breakdown because Jesus interjected, "Be not afraid, only believe" (verse 36). In the face of death, do you become fearful or lose faith?

No matter how prepared we think we are, death has a way of catching us off guard and

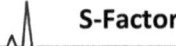

throwing us for a loop. For this reason, the five words Jesus spoke to Jairus were life savers. They breathed life back into Jairus' spirit. He might not have known what Jesus was going to do, but he followed Him in faith.

God always speaks life into our dead circumstances. Are you receiving the words He is speaking to you? Jairus believed and led Jesus to his house where his friends and family were mourning his daughter's death. Jesus told the weepers to leave and followed Jairus and his wife into their daughter's room where she laid dead on her bed. Alone with the parents, Jesus said, "'Talitha cumi;' which is, being interpreted, 'Damsel, I say unto thee, arise'" (verse 41).

At once, the little girl arose from her bed and began to walk around. The Bible declares that everyone who heard the news or saw the young girl alive was astonished by the miracle. With the words "Talitha cumi," Jesus turned Jairus' sorrow into joy. Jairus' determination saved his daughter's life and sent a message to future generations.

The message is "Sorrow doesn't stop death. It stops life. Worrying doesn't take away tomorrow's troubles. It takes away today's peace." Jairus could've stayed home in despair and watched his daughter take her last breath. He could've given up hope. But with a mustard-seed faith, he left home and went looking for Jesus. This is an example for each of us to follow when facing death or difficult circumstances.

We don't have to sit in grief awaiting the moment of doom. Jairus' miracle should encourage us to seek Jesus and plead with Him even while we anticipate or face death. We should pursue Jesus because He has "the keys of hell and of death" (Revelation 1:18, KJV). We can rely on the promise that "God sent not his Son into the world to condemn the world; but that the world through Him might be saved" (John 3:17, KJV).

## S-Factor

Jesus ensured our salvation by leaving heaven, living 33 ½ years on earth, and giving His life on Calvary's cross. No matter the source of our anguish—death, past failures or current trials—the solution is Jesus. Regardless of how weak we get; we can find strength in Jesus. Relying completely on Him, we can overcome a child's death like Janet, stand firm and speak up for our child's life like the harlot, or move forward in faith despite receiving heart-breaking news like Jairus.

The harlot's and Jairus' stories ended on a happy note because God answered their prayers right away and saved their children. Despite much prayer, God did not save Janet's baby. He did, however, manifest His power in a remarkable way. Less than two years after losing her baby, Janet gave birth to a beautiful baby girl which brought much joy to the family. The news also gave hope to those who had mourned with Janet and her family.

Janet's experience reminds us that we may experience sorrow because of this sinful world, but knowing we have a loving Savior, makes all the difference. With Jesus, we're able to face trials and anticipate the miracles that lie ahead. In the future, Christ promises to wipe away our tears and there'll be no more sorrow, mourning, crying or pain. I am happily anticipating this time. Are you?

*Dear Jesus, You know that death has a fatal sting and it brings despair. Whether it's the death of an estranged father or our children, the pain can be unbearable. In the face of sorrow, give us supernatural strength to hold on to our sanity and faith. As we move on by faith, Your name will be glorified, and doubters will know You're real. We want to stand in the gap for those being overpowered by grief. We pray that You "console those who mourn in Zion [and all over the world], to give them beauty for ashes, the oil of joy for mourning, the*

**S-Factor**

*garment of praise for the spirit of heaviness"
(Isaiah 61:3, NKJV). Thank you, Lord, for hearing
and answering our prayer.*

**Bridgette Bastien**

# S-Factor 6: Secrets and Schemes

The hypocrite's mask mesmerized us. You should've seen its dramatically shaped eye sockets, exaggerated facial expressions, and untamed animal hair. Spellbound, my family and I sat captive for hours as we were entertained by a one-man puppet show in New York City.

> "For God will bring every work into judgment, including every secret thing, whether good or evil."
>
> Ecclesiastes 12:14

During that show, we learned that in Ancient Greece, actors, also called hypocrites, wore masks to represent different characters. These masks were impressive from an artistic point of view. Some were molded out of wood, leather, gold, or silver; others were fashioned from porcelain and painted with bright reds, oranges, blues, and greens. Many masks extenuated a character flaw, such as fear, joy, sadness, happiness, or anger.

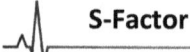 S-Factor

Despite their artistic expression, the masks' main purpose was to hide the person behind it and present a caricature. The concealing of one's true self was acceptable in the theaters of Ancient Greece. The actor flawlessly transitioned from one character to the next during the puppet show. With each new mask, he changed his voice, mannerisms, and stature.

We knew the actor would be wearing masks, but once the show began, we were so wrapped up in the music and drama that the masks took on lives of their own. We forgot his face, and the characters became real. After the show, the performer spent some time explaining the power of masks. He shared that he often loses himself and becomes his masked persona.

Like this actor recreating the stories of Ancient Greece, we also walk around masked every day. Many of our masks are invisible, but no less dramatic. Some people intentionally put on a mask to face the world. Sometimes the mask is used to portray a socially acceptable

**Bridgette Bastien**

character. Have you ever wondered, if people like the real you or the mask you put on every day? Often times, our masks are used as camouflage, enabling us to fit into certain crowds.

At other times, it hides the pain and fears that crush our souls. There are even times when masks conceal secrets, hide skeletons in our closets, or cover up our diabolic and selfish schemes. Tragically, some of us wear masks for such a long time that our real character cannot be recognized, even when our masks are off. Are you wearing an invisible mask right now?

Masks are very effective in covering up who we truly are. But while we can hide from others, we cannot hide from God. God knows our every thought, and He sees past the camouflage to our very core. He urges us to come to Him as we are, not how we want to be perceived by others. Salvation requires that we allow Jesus into our hearts and surrender our fears and faults to Him.

## S-Factor

We cannot be saved if we don't remove our masks and be fully transparent. Our masks may be attractive, but if they don't reflect Jesus' character, they're repulsive to God. Our masks may be expensive, but if they weren't molded in the Creator's image, they're worthless. If you're unsure or don't want to admit ever wearing a mask, the Bible story of Judah and Tamar is for you.

Recorded in Genesis 38, this story tells of a descendant of Abraham named Judah. He had two sons, Er and Onan. Er was wicked and God took his life. As part of Onan's brotherly duty, he married Tamar, Er's widow. Onan was supposed to have children with Tamar and guarantee his dead brother an heir. Onan was willing to have sex with Tamar, but refused to extend his brother's legacy. He "emitted [his semen] on the ground" (Genesis 38:9) instead of fulfilling his duty to impregnate Tamar. Onan, also suffered the same destiny—death—as his brother because of his evil schemes.

The death of both sons was devastating for Judah. He unjustly blamed his sons' death on Tamar instead of their rebellion against God. Judah put together his own scheme, promising Tamar that she could marry his third son once he came of age. Judah had no intentions of fulfilling this promise and sent Tamar to live with her parents until the appointed time.

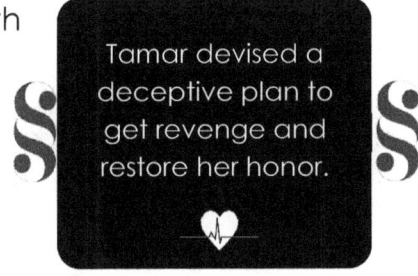

Tamar devised a deceptive plan to get revenge and restore her honor.

After years of waiting, Tamar realized that Judah wasn't going to keep his promise. In desperation, Tamar decided to take matters in her own hands. The Bible says Tamar, "Took off her widow's garments, covered herself with a veil and wrapped herself, and sat in an open place which was on the way to Timnah; for she saw that Shelah was grown, and she was not given to him as a wife" (Genesis 38:13, 14). Instead of relying on God, Tamar devised a deceptive plan to get revenge and restore her honor.

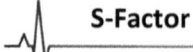 S-Factor

First, she denied who she was by removing her widow's clothing. Second, she covered herself in a veil. When it comes to masking, it is not enough to remove a few items. We must completely strip or hide ourselves. Third, Tamar put on a new character by wrapping herself up in a disguise. Her physical mask took on a life of its own that even Tamar's closest family members didn't recognize her.

Tamar's mask wasn't the only one decorated with dark secrets and sensual schemes. Judah's flawed character made him susceptiable to Tamar's plot. He appeared to be a "righteaous man," but he must have solicited prostitues regularly when he went up to Timnah to shear sheep. If this wasn't his normal behavior, Tamar wouldn't have been able to lure him.

The Bible says, when Judah saw her in disguise, "He thought she was a harlot, because she had covered her face. Then he turned to her by the way, and said, 'Please let me come in to you;' for he did not know that she was his daughter-in-law" (Genesis 38:15-16). Tamar's mask was indeed captivating and powerful. She cunningly used it to seduce her father-in-law, thus ensuring his demise.

After they slept together, Tamar left Judah's bed, returned home, removed her veil, and replaced her widow's clothing. As she removed her disguise, or mask, I can imagine it also ripping away her dignity, leaving her feeling empty and sad. Tamar was successful in her scheme, but at what cost? There's always a price to pay when we plot and scheme instead of trusting the Lord to fight our battles.

Judah also paid a high price about three months after his rendezvous. With righteous indignation, he decided to be Tamar's judge, juror, and executioner threatening to have her killed because she was pregnant. However, his own signet, cord, and staff became the irrefutable evidence of his unrighteousness. His mask was ripped off by this evidence. His secret habit became his public shame. Judah's fall from

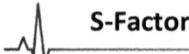 **S-Factor**

grace reminds us that there are always consequences to sin.

Like Judah and Tamar, many of us wear masks just to make it through the day. We put our masks on as soon as we wake up, before we leave our homes, when we get to work and even to attend church. We sometimes decorate them to camouflage who we really. Our professional masks often portray ambitious, confident, and hard-working employees even on the days when we don't feel this way. Our religious masks present righteous, loving, and faithful followers of Christ even though we are sinners struggling to make it through each day.

We fake it because our bosses, colleagues, pastors and fellow parishioners wouldn't accept the real us, or at least that's what we believe. We fake it because we've seen others get penalized, marginalized, or disfellowshipped when they don't.

On the other hand, some people get rewarded for being "the best actors" based on their professional or religious masks. Those who choose not to fake it, or don't know how to, often won't "fit" within the confines of certain churches, communities, corporations, or the larger culture.

In countries like Hong Kong or Tokyo, wearing masks for health reasons and safety have been the cultural norm for several years. Some places in the United States, didn't mandate wearing a physical mask in public until the recent rise of COVID-19. Now we must wear masks whenever we step inside a store or business, or even outside of our homes. "These masks are for our safety and protection," the experts say. I can't refute that fact, but I've learned that wearing masks, whether visible or invisible, have psychological effects.

Those who wear them often feel like they're suffocating, losing their perspective, or being judged by the world. Those who see others

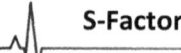 **S-Factor**

wearing masks subconsciously deduce that they're unhealthy, deceptive, or dangerous. Furthermore, authenticity is often lost when we willingly or unwillingly conceal ourselves behind masks whether for safety, secrets, or schemes.

Isn't it ironic that even at home, where we should be genuine, many of us wear invisible masks? We just switch from the professional or public masks to personal ones. We pretend everything is wonderful when we're hurting and falling apart. The struggle to be the perfect mom, dad, sibling, friend, husband, wife, son, and daughter forces us to wear masks. We say, "Yes" when we want to say, "No." We act like Energizer bunnies when we are completely exhausted, or we laugh out loud when we're miserable inside.

We wear masks to hide who we are and to live up to the expectations of others—family, friends, or even strangers. It seems easier to wear masks and play different roles than honestly express ourselves at the risk of being misunderstood or disliked by others. Many of us don't really understand how dangerous wearing masks can be. When we wear them long enough, we eventually become what we pretend to be while losing our true identity.

The world says "fake it 'til you make it," but Jesus says "be real to God, yourself and others." Jesus wants us to remove our masks and put on His character. Like Moses who spent 40 days with God and was enlightened by His glory, we need a transformational experience with God. The Shekinah glory of God left a divine glow on Moses which was so bright that it prevented the people of Israel from looking directly at his face (Exodus 34: 28-35).

It's impossible not to be changed after being in the presence of God or to reflect His light after spending quality time with Him. When we walk and talk with God, we willingly remove our superficial masks and allow ourselves to be fully consumed by His character. Rather than switching masks based on the occasion, we

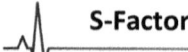 **S-Factor**

need to keep on the character of Christ and pray to have an experience like Moses.

When Moses came down from the mountain, He had to veil his face. This was not to conceal himself or implement a devious plan, like Tamar, but rather to protect the Israelites. The people couldn't stand in the afterglow of God's glory. We can't stand in God's presence when we're hiding secrets and planning schemes. Moses covered his face in the presence of the people "but whenever Moses went in before the Lord to speak with Him, he would take the veil off" (Exodus 34: 33, 34). Likewise, we must remove all our veils and masks before communing with God.

When we pray, we cannot hide behind our past, polish our tarnished present, or disguise our plans. God knows us better than we know ourselves. He requires that we come to Him as we are—whether clean or filthy, happy or sad, rich or poor, whole or broken. It's only when we seek God with a sincere heart that He is able to change us. He'll alter our body, mind, and soul according to His Word. After being in God's presence, there has to be a conversion of the heart. Some people will be drawn to us because of this change, and others will be repelled by God's glory.

Our primary focus should always be reflecting God's brilliant, radiant glow which requires that we remove our masks. Each day with sincere prayer and humility, I am chiseling off my mask one ceramic piece at a time. Masks are appropriate for Greek theaters or children's puppet shows but they're not fitting for facing life's realities.

Are you wearing a mask to hide your secrets or camouflage some deceptive schemes? Are you wearing a mask because the world doesn't accept you as you are? If so, join me in removing it. Remove the mask and know that whatever flaws we see when it's off, they can be made perfect in Christ.

## S-Factor

**S-Factor Prayer**

Lord Jesus, we have been told for years that we aren't sociable, smart, or successful without our masks. This perception makes us fearful to leave home without our disguises. We are even scared to have those closest to us experience who were really are without our masks. Our desire is to reflect Your character. We may have to wear physical masks for our safety, but give us the courage to remove our invisible masks that are slowly taking our breath away. We need You to expose the hidden secrets that are tearing us apart from the inside out. Consume us with Your glory and Your character so that when others see us, they see You.

# S-Factor 7: Seventy times Seven

Secrets and schemes led to our first real fight! We were together for almost two years and never had a full-blown feud like this one. There were no physical blows, but our words were just as hard-hitting as a punch or kick.

> "Love suffers long and is kind; love does not envy; love does not parade itself, is not puffed up; does not behave rudely, does not seek its own, is not provoked, thinks no evil."
>
> 1 Corinthians 13:4-5

We are both doing a lot of talking, but we were not listening to each other. In the end, I tried over and over again to state my case, but Dre wanted to hear none of it. He wanted me gone and made that clear as he pushed me out of the living room, down the long flight of stairs, and through the front door. Grabbing onto the staircase for balance, my mind raced with many thoughts, but I couldn't seem to articulate any of

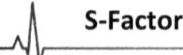 **S-Factor**

them. I stumbled as he shoved me through the door; and my eardrums vibrated as he yelled, "Get out!" and slammed the door.

Leaving that tumultuous situation should've been liberating, but the summer heat of Brooklyn, New York, mixed with Dre's harsh words had me trapped physically and mentally. I never thought our relationship would end this way, and his dark brown eyes conveyed the same message. Before this fight, we had some great times—hours of honest and heart-felt conversations, unforgettable couple's trips and adventures, as well as memorable celebrations with friends and family.

The dreams we had about a bright future together vanished, and instead, dark memories and broken hearts lingered. I tried to garner enough strength to walk away, but my knees felt weak and I could barely move my legs. All I could do was stand outside facing the brown wooden door that was just slammed in my face.

**Bridgette Bastien**

The sound of that door crushed any hopes we had of reconciliation. I stood in that spot for a while trying to find the strength to make it to my car and drive far away from our relationship. Dre and I both walked away that day without speaking to each other for decades. However, those enraged words uttered during our argument replayed again and again in my mind.

Over the next year, whenever they would flood my mind, sadness filled my heart. It's unfortunate how selfish actions and harsh words can turn bliss into bitterness. Harsh words like "Get out of my life," "I never want to see you again," or "I hate you" often lay the foundation for a lifetime of brokenness, pain, and resentment.

Each one of us has either said those words or have been on the receiving end of them. Whether we are the receiver or deliverer of such cruel words, there is always a lasting effect. Words are powerful. Words can either inspire, heal, and build up, or they can discourage, harm, and tear down.

## S-Factor

During my childhood, I believed the nursery rhyme that said, "Sticks and stones may break my bones, but words will never hurt me." You may have also sung these words and believed them. As an adult, I can assure everyone that this nursery rhyme is far from the truth because "death and life are in the power of the tongue" (Proverbs 18:21). Words do hurt. Often times, the impact of words uttered in anger can last longer than the pain from a physical blow.

Cruel words can destroy friendships and relationships. Many relationships become toxic because of betrayal, abuse, abandonment, adultery, fornication, lies, secrets, schemes, or miscommunication. When relationships come to an end, some people scream and spurt angry words, while others remain silent even if their hearts are boiling with contempt. Are you a screamer or the silent type?

I have always been the silent type. When I am extremely upset, I shut down, withdraw within myself and brew over whatever is making me mad. This may not be the best approach, but it's definitely a defense mechanism that has served me well in the past. Unfortunately, holding onto my anger and malice over the years as well as suppressing hurt from past relationships have resulted in me embracing the spirit of unforgiveness.

Unforgiveness and I became close friends for many years. We hung out together, laughing and talking for hours. We reminisced about the past and made a pact to forever hold others accountable for their actions. We never discussed my accountability, or the root cause of some issues, because that was irrelevant in our relationship. While God was telling me to deal with my emotional baggage, unforgiveness told me to neatly pack my memories—good and bad—into several boxes and then label them, "Past-life. Do not open."

I followed unforgiveness' advice, stacked those boxes high in my emotional closet, and closed the door behind me with no intentions of looking back. When God was telling me to repent, pray for forgiveness, and to forgive those who hurt me, unforgiveness told me something else. It encouraged me to ignore my woes, close those relationship suitcases, and move on with my life. God wanted to save me, while unforgiveness was suffocating me.

I couldn't see it years ago, but the spirit of unforgiveness didn't have my best interest in mind. Do you currently have a relationship with unforgiveness or are you considering dating it? I urge you not to entertain such a heartless companion. Unlike the Holy Spirit, the spirit of unforgiveness does not comfort. It does not offer hope. It's more like a broken glass; the tighter we hold it and the more we squeeze it, the deeper our cuts, and the longer our wounds take to heal.

God reminds us in the Bible that it is He "who forgiveth all thine iniquities; who healeth all thy diseases" (Psalm 103:3, KJV) and He calls us to "be ye kind one to another, tenderhearted, forgiving one another, even as God for Christ's sake hath forgiven you" (Ephesians 4:32, KJV). Life is about healing and growing. This is impossible without forgiveness.

I couldn't heal and/or truly move forward when the shattered pieces of my heart were crying out from the past. When we don't deal with our past, it'll inevitably show up in our present and sometimes even threaten our future. Knowing that our past can sometimes destroy our future, it's natural to never want to look back. "Remember Lot's wife" (Luke 17:32, KJV) who turned into a pillar of salt and died because she looked back. I was determined to never look back and became content with disobeying God's direction to repent and reconcile with my past.

I was shocked when my past showed up in my present. I didn't know how to react or how to process all those buried emotions. It took some time for me to realize that this was God's divine will and timing. When Dre and I reconnected, we were both open to embrace the power of forgiveness. We were now parents and successful professionals who had grown immensely over the years through God's grace.

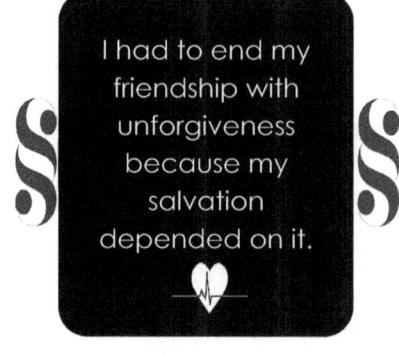

The purpose of our reunion was to restore and build up our faith, not to destroy or tear it down. After reconnecting with my past, I wanted to turn back the hands of time and un-do the pain and suffering. God was urging me to open my emotional storage room, clean out the mess, sincerely forgive myself and Dre, then move forward—free and spiritually enlightened.

I had to end my friendship with unforgiveness because my salvation depended on it. The Bible says, "For if you forgive men their trespasses, your heavenly Father will also forgive you. But if you do not forgive men their trespasses, neither will your Father forgive your trespasses" (Matthew 6:14, 15). This is a very sobering text because of its conditional promise. God will forgive us if we first forgive others.

I shudder to think that I had been living in a state of unforgiveness for almost two decades. Every day, I had been limiting God and His desire to forgive me because I was unwilling to face the past and give up the hurt. It's selfish to ask for forgiveness while being vengeful towards others. It's unrealistic to pray to God for forgiveness, but refuse to pardon others. Are you living in a state of unforgiveness?

Matthew 18:23-35 recaps the story of an unforgiving servant. This servant owed the king millions of dollars (based on today's monetary system) but couldn't afford to pay it. The king wanted to put him in jail, then sell his family and property in order to cover the debt. The servant fell to his knees and begged the king for mercy. The compassionate king forgave his debt. God also cancels our debts once we accept His gift of salvation.

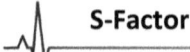 **S-Factor**

After leaving the king's presence, the unforgiving servant saw someone who owed him a few hundred dollars. He choked the man and demanded payment on the spot. When the man begged for mercy, the unforgiving servant had no compassion, and had the man thrown in jail. The people in the community were appalled at his cruelty. The king heard about the servant's lack of compassion and decided to reinstate the servant's debt and imprison him.

We are not called to be unforgiving servants. Forgiving others can be hard, but it's the key that unlocks God's mercy toward us. I had to pray long and hard for a forgiving heart. A heart that'll first forgive my shortcomings and won't rejoice in punishing others for their past mistakes. A heart that'll look beyond someone's flaws and willing offer the gift of reconciliation.

God offers us this gift every day and expects us to extend the same courtesy. I've heard people say, "They need to apologize to me first" or "They will never forgive me." God doesn't care whose fault it is; He expects us to repair every broken breach with an open and compassionate heart.

This is clear in Jesus' response when Peter asked, "Lord, how oft shall my brother sin against me, and I forgive him? till seven times? Jesus saith unto him, I say not unto thee, until seven times: but, until seventy times seven" (Matthew 18:21, 22, KJV). Notice Jesus didn't ask Peter to relive how his brother sinned against him. Jesus also didn't say, "Forgive him as many times as he forgives you." Jesus sets the bar at a heavenly level by saying, "Forgive seventy times seven."

It takes divine intervention to forgive someone four hundred and ninety times. Only a heart full of humility and love can move past the hurt, forget an adversarial interaction, and embrace someone who has caused immense pain. Have you forgiven your spouse, parents, family members, children, ex-partner, friends, and colleagues seventy times seven times yet?

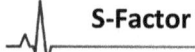 **S-Factor**

Forgiveness is a decision we make to release someone from the feelings of anger we have toward them. Forgiveness is a heart matter, not just utterance from the lips. We often say the words "I forgive you," but then rehash the person's wrong-doings every chance we get. We've all made mistakes, hurt those in our lives (intentionally and unintentionally), or spoke unimaginable words in the heat of the moment.

By focusing only on mistakes or shortcomings, we'll never be able to completely heal or find inner peace. Sometimes, the most difficult thing to do is to forgive "oneself." We may forgive others, but continue to beat up on ourselves. God also expects us to forgive ourselves at least four hundred and ninety times. Self-forgiveness is difficult, but possible through Christ. We can and should release ourselves from guilt and shame.

God's love is about forgiveness, sacrifice, patience, and humility. There is no love without forgiveness, and there is no forgiveness without

**Bridgette Bastien**

love. God described Himself when honoring Moses' request to see His face by proclaiming, "The Lord, the Lord God, merciful and gracious, longsuffering, and abounding in goodness and truth; keeping mercy and lovingkindness for thousands, forgiving iniquity and transgression and sin" (Exodus 34:6, 7).

God is a forgiving God, and "there is therefore now no condemnation for those who are in Christ Jesus." (Romans 8:1). Once we ask for forgiveness, repent, and forgive others, we are free from condemnation and can accept the unconditional love offered by Jesus. Love heals all wounds and love conquers all. God wants us to love those whom He has placed in our lives, whether it is for a moment or for many moons.

It is possible for us to break up with unforgiveness and pray to release grudges or malice. It took many months of praying for me to break off my relationship with unforgiveness. Once I slammed the door on unforgiveness, I was

 S-Factor

able to open my heart, forgive myself, and share the gift of forgiveness with Dre. What God has done for me; He will do for you. Are you willing to break up with unforgiveness and, in love, choose to forgive seventy times seven? If you are, God will allow you to overcome the trauma from your past and walk in the newness of life through Christ.

*God, forgive us for falling short of Your expectations. Give us forgiving hearts and humble spirits. We've been hurt by many people, and we've hurt many folks over the years. We no longer want to live in a state of unforgiveness. We know You will not forgive us unless we forgive others. Fill us with your Holy Spirit. We need to absolve our loved ones, even if they don't want to hear from us, or they're no longer here on earth. Humble us. When others ask for forgiveness, we want to grant it with a loving attitude and without exorbitant requirements. Help us, Lord!*

# S-Factor 8: Speck of Sawdust

We all have insecurities, and sometimes they add up to more than seventy times seven. It could be the slant of our eyes, flair of our noses, shape of our

> *"Judge not, that you be not judged. For with what judgment you judge, you will be judged; and with the measure you use, it will be measured back to you."*
>
> *Matthew 7:1, 2*

faces, or length of our hair. Perhaps, it's the size of our breasts, breadth of our shoulders, bulge of our stomachs, or curve of our hips. It may be the span of our buttocks, bow of our legs, arch of our feet, or tone of our skin.

Each of us have looked at our bodies at some point in time and wondered why certain parts couldn't be bigger or smaller, wider or narrower, darker or lighter, shorter or taller. Many of us are dissatisfied with our body image, though not all of us are willing to admit it. Sometimes, this discontentment originates from within us. Our internal voice tells us that we are not good enough, and we don't measure up to our definition of beauty or excellence.

Other times, it comes from external sources. You may have had a childhood filled with negative feedback from parents, siblings, family or friends, years of elementary and high schools' rejections, teasing, and bullying. Perhaps you've tried to measure up to magazine covers, television images, or social media posts, which define beauty in a marginalized way.

All these sources impact how we see ourselves and make it very difficult to recognize beauty when we look in a mirror. A mirror can be a complementary friend or a harsh foe. There are times when we are looking fierce, and a mirror confirms it. There are other times when we are not confident and need a mirror for validation. There are also jolting moments when we think we have it altogether, and a mirror reveals we are a total mess.

**Bridgette Bastien**

Sometimes we try to see beyond our tears, grief, and pain by looking into mirrors. Have you ever stood in front of a mirror attempting to recognize the person staring back at you? Regardless of the shape or size of our mirrors, we can only see our outward appearances. Our reflections only reveal our scars from the past and who we are in the present, but not who we are meant to be in the future.

The Bible is clear, "God created man in His own image; in the image of God He created him; male and female He created them" (Genesis 1:27). No magazine cover, television show, or mirror can ever reflect our true image. Most of the images we see on a daily basis are distorted or marred in some way. It is only through heaven's eyes that we will see a complete picture of ourselves.

We're much more than our red lipsticks, angelic faces, tight jeans, broad shoulders, rugged looks, or button-down shirts. We're more than our scarred faces, blackened eyes,

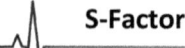 **S-Factor**

smeared make-up, bruised hands, tattered clothes, or raggedy shoes. Pause for a moment and think about how you see yourself. Does your self-evaluation align with God's Word or with someone else's view of you?

We are made in the image of God. Each of us is a tapestry of colorful threads intricately woven together into a complete masterpiece. Those who look at us from afar should see a breathtaking piece of artwork. Those who look at us closely will see the individual threads perfectly intertwined to reflect God's creativity, diversity and uniqueness. We were made in the image of love, perfection, and righteousness.

We were not quickly or clumsily thrown together to patch a hole in the universe. We are not man-made mistakes or here on this earth by happenstance. Whether we were conceived out of love or through rape, born in or out-of-wedlock, supported or deserted by our biological parents, our lives have a purpose. Each fiber of our being was purposefully crafted by the Creator.

Whenever I struggle to see myself through God's eyes, I think of King David's statement: "I will praise thee; for I am fearfully and wonderfully made: marvelous are thy works; and that my soul knoweth right well" (Psalms 139:14, KJV). This verse can be a life-saver for those who believe and proclaim it on a consistent basis. Repeat these words a few times, "I am fearfully and wonderfully made." Doesn't that verse just builds your confidence and make you appreciate who you are?

Often times, people mutilate themselves or commit suicide because of self-hate. Others die trying to change their physical appearance through face lifts, breast implants, Botox shots, butt enhancement, and reduction surgeries. There is no need for us to go to such extremes to be considered beautiful or handsome. God already formed us with His own hands and breathed into us the breath of life (Genesis 2:7).

## S-Factor

We are fearfully and wonderfully made by God. The slant of our eyes, flair of our noses, shape of our faces, breadth of our shoulders, size of our breasts, or bow of our legs are not mistakes. Even those who are born with missing limps or deformities are special in the eyes of God. In fact, every person is unique like a snowflake, fingerprint, and tear.

A snowflake typically displays a delicate, six-fold symmetry. A fingerprint identifies individuals based on a unique pattern of whorls and lines. Even tears of joy and sadness look different under the microscope.[4] We are perfectly made in His likeness, and our uniqueness is not a curse, but a confirmation that God loves diversity. We are God's masterpiece, no matter how we see ourselves.

The next time you look in the mirror, try seeing yourself as God views you. We should find comfort in knowing that God does not dwell on

---

[4] According to photographer Rose-Lynn Fisher in her series *The Topography of Tears* (Published 2017).

our flaws, brokenness, shortcomings, or the speck of sawdust in our eyes. God looks at us through heaven's

eyes and decided we were worth saving.

He sees a flawless body, a strong mind, a loving character, and uplifted spirit because of Jesus' blood. When we view ourselves through heaven's eyes, we are able to break through every self-loathing barrier. When we see others through God's divine lens, we are less likely to judge based on physical appearance or preconceived notions. Unfortunately, prejudice happens in the church as often as it does in the world.

Recently on a conference call, someone—let's refer to her as "Rose"—joined the call while we were discussing the topic of judging others. Rose was blown away by our discussion and soon confessed that she was up all night because of an argument with her son. He was very angry with her and in frustration exclaimed, "I thought you were a Christian!" before hanging up the phone.

These words robbed her of hours of sleep. Rose expressed how upset she was that he would question her Christianity. She thought that her consistent church attendance, regular prayers, and in-depth Bible study should be enough evidence of her Christianity. We could tell by the sorrow in her voice that she was eagerly searching for a resolution to her problem.

When we asked several probing questions about her son's frustration, Rose admitted that she didn't like his current girlfriend. She didn't like the young lady's family background, her life choices, and the unexplainable hold she had on her son. Some parents may be able to relate to Rose's feelings. However, the shocking part of our discussion was when Rose said, "I've never met this young girl."

**Bridgette Bastien**

We were all taken aback that she never met her son's girlfriend in person, but notwithstanding this, she had some unsubstantiated beliefs about who this young woman was. Supposedly, her maternal instinct was the determining factor and she was convinced, "The young lady was not good enough for her son." Rose's prejudice was obvious to everyone on the call, but she couldn't see it. Have you ever wrestled with sin factors that cause pre-judgment?

Rose's son attempted to enlighten her, but to no avail and in anger he questioned her Christianity. Christians are supposed to love others, no matter the person or circumstance. We could hear the anguish in Rose's voice as she struggled with accepting this young woman. We urged Rose not to focus on the speck of sawdust in this young lady's eyes, but to see this young lady through God's eyes. We also cautioned her to not put her son in a position where he must choose between his mom and girlfriend. If given

 S-Factor

that choice, his decision would surely result in resentment and heartache for everyone.

Rose's circumstance is not unique. Most of us are quick to judge without taking time to get to know each other. Jesus witnessed the same prejudice and asked, "Why do you look at the speck of sawdust in your brother's eye and pay no attention to the plank in your own eye? How can you say to your brother, 'Let me take the speck out of your eye,' when all the time there is a plank in your own eye?" (Matthew 7:3, 4). These are tough questions that, as Christians, we must answer.

Although sawdust, a by-product of woodworking operations, can vary in size, it is usually microscopic and very difficult to see with the naked eye. A plank can be any length, but generally is a minimum of 2 inches deep by 8 inches wide. These facts emphasize the profoundness of Jesus' questions. How can we see something small in someone else's eye if our vision is blocked by a 2"x8" slab of wood?

We cannot clearly see others if our visions are obstructed by pride, envy, wrath, laziness, greed, gluttony, or lust. If we cannot see, why do we so easily judge? The Bible says, "So then each of us shall give account of himself to God. Therefore, let us not judge one another anymore, but rather resolve this, not to put a stumbling block or a cause to fall in our brother's way" (Romans 14:12, 13).

It takes a mature person to honestly evaluate why they judge others. Many times, our prejudices arise before we get to know each other's character. In Rose's case, she was using her maternal instincts to marginalize and stereotype her son's girlfriend. Instincts are often right, but not always, and are sometimes influenced by our past experiences. Instincts can be an invaluable armor of protection or unnecessary barricade.

Remember, love doesn't judge. Love doesn't belittle. Love will remove the plank from our eyes first and then the speck of sawdust from

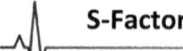 **S-Factor**

our brothers' eyes. We are supposed to live a life characterized by love. We are called to uplift those around us and not to be a stumbling block.

When we stand before God, we'll have to give an account of our thoughts, words, and deeds. If we intentionally cause anyone to stumble and do not repent from our sins, we may hear Jesus say, "I never knew you; depart from Me, you who practice lawlessness!" (Matthew 7:23). These are frightening words to put on paper much less to hear uttered from Christ's mouth.

It's a challenge, but we can make a conscious effort to focus on each other's forte rather than faults. Until we do this, harsh words, resentment, and sleepless nights will continue to fill our lives. I pray that Rose begins to look at others through heaven's eyes. I have no doubt that if she does, she will see their beauty, strength, and perfection through Christ.

**Bridgette Bastien**

I pray that we'll also embrace the beauty in others and graciously accept how we look regardless of what's represented on magazine covers, television images, or in social media posts. I encourage you to look at yourself through heaven's eyes. When we see God clearly and acknowledge that we are all made in His image, we will celebrate our chiseled chest and voluptuous curves, or lack thereof, and even delight in our differences.

 *Jesus, I've learned that instead of finding the speck of sawdust in my brother or sister's eye, I need to remove the plank from my own eye. Help us, Lord, to see ourselves and other people through Your eyes. We know that our differences shine brilliantly through Your divine lens. Our brightness, as well as how we perceive the light shining from others, depends on our closeness to You, the true Light. Draw us closer God. We want to focus on You and celebrate how You've made and molded us in Your image.*

## S-Factor 9: Seeing the Spirit

We may not be able to see a speck of sawdust, but God's Word is visible to all who believe. God spoke and the world

> "'Not by might nor by power, but by My Spirit,' says the Lord of hosts."
>
> Zechariah 4:6

was created in six days from nothing. The Bible says, "In the beginning God created the heavens and earth. The earth was without form, and void; and darkness was on the face of the deep. And the Spirit of God was hovering over the face of the waters" (Genesis 1:1-3).

God spoke and everything changed. He commanded and what had no form took shape, what was empty became filled, and darkness gave way to light. Before God spoke a word, the Holy Spirit moved or "hovered" over the face of the waters. The Spirit's movement might have appeared motionless to the naked eye, but it was preparing the way for God. Often times, the Spirit is moving in our lives, but we can't see it.

We don't perceive it because life is chaotic or we are not focused on God. Perhaps, we don't realize it because we're more concerned with taking selfies and getting social media "likes" than hearing the Holy Spirit's utterance. Three years ago, I wasn't aware that the Holy Spirit was moving in my life. I wrestled with God to do my will versus His. We grappled for months, but to no avail.

During this season, I felt that the Spirit of God had left me. I struggled to pray, fast, and study the Bible consistently. I was in darkness; light was hiding from me. Everything I touched seemed to wither instead of grow. I was working crazy hours, but my projects were yielding minimal results. Despite my best efforts and spending ungodly hours strategizing and executing on my professional and personal plan, I was not achieving my goals.

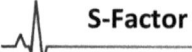 **S-Factor**

I was spending less time with my family and felt overwhelmed by guilt. I wanted to get out of this quagmire, but didn't know how to on my own. I began to re-evaluate my value in life. Have you ever contemplated your purpose or tried to sum up your value, but everything added up to zero? I couldn't see the Holy Spirit hovering over my dark moments, but He was there all along.

One morning, the Spirit did more than just hover—He moved supernaturally in my life. I was listening to gospel music via YouTube when a sermon "popped up" in my queue. I swiped past the sermon and returned to my music. The next day, I tried listening to my playlist again, but only a sermon called "Don't Quit, Anything Can Happen," from a renowned pastor would play. I was annoyed at first, then reluctantly, decided to listen to it.

God spoke to me through that sermon. The message was powerful! I sat in my car for over 30 minutes amazed by how God works. The pastor

**Bridgette Bastien**

focused on Joseph's life journey and him being in prison for two years. He also covered most of the dark areas in my life—the stresses of work, being under-valued, the desire to quit, the feeling of hopelessness, and the questions I had; did God know that I was struggling, and furthermore, did He care at all?

The Holy Spirit moved, and God spoke through the sermon. It reaffirmed God's love for me, His saving grace, and His purpose for my life, despite the pain that I was experiencing. Although the sermon gave me some hope, my spirit remained defeated. I went to bed that night worrying and contemplating the different challenges I would face the next day.

The following morning, I prayed longer than usual, but it seemed as though my prayers were not getting through to heaven. I felt like they were hitting the ceiling, bouncing back, and landing on the floor. I got off my knees and walked upstairs with my head hanging low. In my heart I asked, "God, are you there, and do you even care?"

Stepping into the shower, I pondered why God had deserted me. The thought didn't quite leave my mind, when suddenly, my youngest daughter, Elise, burst into the bathroom.

"Mommy, do you want to hear my memory verse for school?" she asked.

"Not right now baby, why don't you share it with me later?" I said. At that moment, all I wanted was peace and quiet.

She boldly responded, "No, I am going to share it with you now. Genesis 28:15 says, 'Behold, I am with you and will keep you wherever you go, and will bring you back to this land; for I will not leave you until I have done what I have spoken to you.'"

I stood in the shower speechless as her words vibrated through the shower doors and penetrated my heart and soul. I couldn't find the

**Bridgette Bastien**

words to express my appreciation, but tears of gratitude flowed down my cheeks. She broke my silence by exclaiming, "I'll tell it to you again when you get out of the shower," then disappeared as quickly as she had come.

In the midst of my doom and gloom, the Spirit hovered, and God spoke to me. He made it clear through the pastor, and through Elise, that He'd heard my prayers. He wouldn't leave me until He had fulfilled His promises. One of His many promises that I've now personally claimed is found in Isaiah 43:19: "Behold, I will do a new thing, now it shall spring forth; shall you not know it? I will even make a road in the wilderness and rivers in the desert."

I didn't know then what this novel thing was, and God didn't reveal it right away. Yet, I had an unexplainable hunger and thirst for His Word. I was determined to understand this new thing. I diligently searched the Bible for the new things—mankind, rainbow, and virgin birth—God

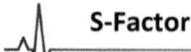 **S-Factor**

created on the earth. It was during my studies that I rediscovered the creation story.

During creation, God did something new. Darkness gave way to light, trees and mountains appeared from nowhere, streams and rivers flowed, animals of every kind mingled in harmony, and man became a living soul from dust. The possibility of what God can do is limitless. Think for a moment—what new thing could God be planning to do in your life?

He says, He is doing something NEW. According to the Oxford English Dictionary, "new" means "not existing before; not made before, not introduced before, or discovered recently." This new thing will be so phenomenal that we'll sing a new song. Many people will hear it and God will be praised for His miraculous and marvelous power.

God asked, "Shall you not know it?" The question is a rhetorical one. God wants to ensure that we will give credit where credit is due. As His children, we have a tendency to cry out to God during trials, but afterward, we give credit to others. We thank the doctors for healing us, but shun God, the Great Physician. We thank our family and friends for helping us pay our bills, but overlook God's endless provisions. We thank our bosses for the raise or promotion, but slight God who owns the "cattle on a thousand hills" (Psalms 50:10).

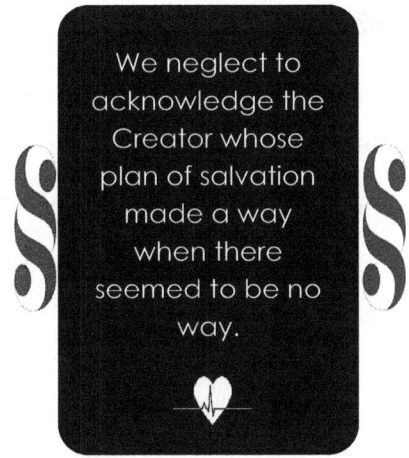

> We neglect to acknowledge the Creator whose plan of salvation made a way when there seemed to be no way.

We neglect to acknowledge the Creator whose plan of salvation made a way when there seemed to be no way. God promises to create a new thing from nothing through the Holy Spirit. Depending on our circumstances, it may be a road in the wilderness or rivers in the desert. Can you imagine the dry ground thirsting for springs of water? Can you hear the rushing waters serenading the hot sand? In a dry, harsh land

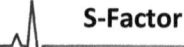

where nothing is growing, God will say, "Let there be rivers." They'll burst forth to create and sustain life. This is not impossible; God has done this before. He provided water from a rock on two different occasions during Biblical times.

In Exodus 17:6, God said to Moses, "Behold, I will stand before you there on the rock in Horeb; and you shall strike the rock, and water will come out of it, that the people may drink." The Israelites were in a dire situation in the wilderness, but God used Moses to provide water for them. In Numbers 20:11, "Moses lifted his hand and struck the rock twice with his rod; and water came out abundantly, and the congregation and their animals drank." Moses did not follow God's direction when he hit the rock twice, but God still supplied the Israelites needs.

Are you wandering through a spiritual desert, thirsting for living water, and praying for a change? You're not alone and there's hope. Despite going through a dry spiritual season, I held onto God's promise and began anticipating the new things He would do in my life. Once my perspective changed, I could hear God speaking and I could see the Spirit moving.

A few months after listening to that sermon and hearing my daughter's declaration, I accepted a new job with a team that valued my professional experience. I was appointed to a new church leadership position that better aligned with my passion, and I started a new prayer ministry to help those trying to overcome life's challenges.

God worked all things together for my good, and for His glory! The Holy Spirit is hovering over your situation. Can you see Him moving? God is speaking directly to your circumstances. Can you hear Him? We may not always see or hear the Lord in the midst of our madness, but we have to live by faith—believing that God will do for us what He did for the Israelites during their wilderness experience.

## S-Factor

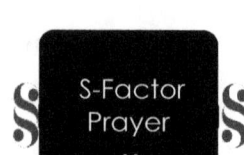

*Holy Spirit, we see You moving in our circumstances. We can feel Your presence in our present chaos. Our doubts and fears disappear when You are present. Our confidence and faith grow stronger when we experience new things in our lives. Thank You for the reminder that You can create order out of confusion and provide light in the midst of darkness. We see Your light, Holy Spirit, direct our paths, we pray.*

**Bridgette Bastien**

# S-Factor 10: Speak, Savior

When was the last time you saw the Holy Spirit move, or heard the voice of the Lord? I'll never forget when God spoke to me and saved my daughter's life.

> "Out of heaven He let you hear His voice, that He might instruct you; on earth He showed you His great fire, and you heard His words out of the midst of the fire."
>
> Deuteronomy 4:36

It was in 2009 during the world-wide H1N1 (swine flu) pandemic. Most people were on edge or in despair, similar to how life is nowadays due to the COVID-19 pandemic. Some folks wore disposable face masks to protect themselves and many took other precautions, like washing hands with antibacterial soap and staying away from anyone who may be sick.

My daughter was almost a year old at the time and we were living in corporate housing in Massachusetts. The work week was often busy,

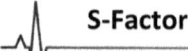 **S-Factor**

but we usually spent our Sundays relaxing around the house or exploring local playgrounds. That last Sunday in May, everything was going great until, out of nowhere, our daughter became clingy and was acting lethargic. Within one hour, her fever spiked over 102°F.

As new parents, Paul and I had no clue what to do. We lived in a brand-new neighborhood with no friends or family nearby. We also had no idea where the closest hospital was to our house. In a word, we were helpless. While we contemplated what to do, my daughter's crying intensified, and then she began throwing up.

It was a scene right out of the movie, *The Exorcist,* except with puking and screaming. We anxiously tried to catch her vomit with our hands, but it was coming at us so fast that it rendered our efforts meaningless. Paul yelled over the screaming, "What should we do?" By this time, Emily was covered in vomit and hysterically crying. My hubby and I just stared at each other.

**Bridgette Bastien**

*Take off her clothes. Get a cold wet rag and wipe her down with the rag. Keep the cold rag on her forehead and then just hold her.* Where did those words come from? God was speaking to me in His still small voice! I began yelling the exact instructions to Paul. He raced back and forth between the living room and bathroom with the cool washcloth. We did everything God said to do, and ten minutes later (although it felt like an eternity), Emily's fever had dropped.

We quickly got dressed, jumped into our vehicle and dashed to the nearest hospital. We burst through the Emergency Room doors, holding our exhausted and almost lifeless daughter. They checked us in quickly and, because of her age, found us a room within a few minutes. As we sat in the room rocking our baby, thoughts of sickness and death haunted me.

*I can't lose my baby. I can't lose my baby.* I kept repeating these words in my mind. The

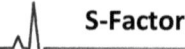 **S-Factor**

doctor came in and interrupted my thoughts, but only to share the horrific news. "Mom and dad, I know it's been a tough day," said the doctor. "Emily might have the swine flu based on her symptoms, but we need to run more tests to be sure."

I was in shock and could only utter, "What?"

The doctor continued, "We'll watch her for a few hours and give her some medication." The look on our faces must have told the story of despair, because the doctor tried to comfort us. "Don't worry," he said. "You are here now, and she'll be fine." He then rose from the tan and brown floral-patterned chair and walked toward the door to leave.

Suddenly, he paused, looked back at us, and said, "Whenever your baby gets a fever, you should take off her clothes, and wipe her down with a wet cloth. Keep the cold cloth on her forehead and make her as comfortable as possible." These were almost the exact

**Bridgette Bastien**

instructions I received from God a few hours earlier. As the doctor spoke these words, Paul turned, stared at me in disbelief, and asked, "How did you know what to do?"

"God told me," I said pointing to the sky. The doctor smiled at us and then left the room just as quietly as he had entered it a few moments earlier.

This was the first, but definitely not the last time God spoke to me regarding our oldest daughter's health. He did it again when Emily was three years old and our youngest daughter was a few months old. It was just us girls at home because my hubby was on a business trip.

We were all fast asleep. Amid my deep sleep, I heard someone say, "Wake up! Wake up! The baby!" I opened my eyes and looked over at Elise who was in a co-sleeper next to me. She appeared fine. I stayed where I was while in a sleepy daze. As I drifted back to sleep, I heard the voice again: "Wake up! Wake up! The baby!"

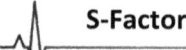 ## S-Factor

I was out of it and very confused because even with my eyes half opened, I could see that baby Elise was sleeping peacefully. As I closed my eyes again, I heard the voice say, "Go, check on the baby!"

The sense of urgency in the voice snatched me from sleep and propelled me into Emily's room. As I turned on the light and touched her little arms, I became fully awake. She was burning up with a fever and struggling to breathe. Her slow panting and whimpering pierced my maternal heart.

I grabbed the thermometer and gently held it under her arm. It flew to 103.5°F within a few seconds. I remembered the divine instructions from a few years previous and immediately began wiping her down with a cold cloth and giving her medication to reduce her fever. Though I wasn't a new parent anymore, my heart pounded just the same.

**Bridgette Bastien**

I frantically called the after-hours emergency service for our pediatrician's office. Speaking to the nurse, she advised me to rush my baby to the hospital if her temperature didn't drop below 101°F within 5-10 minutes.

Crying uncontrollably, it hit me—God saved her again

I sat on the floor in the hallway, rocking Emily in my arms. While crying uncontrollably, it hit me—God saved her again. I wiped away my tears with the back of my hand, dried my damp chest with the edge of my nightgown and began praising God. I couldn't help repeating these words, "Thank you, God for saving my baby. Thank you, God. Thank you, God."

I was thankful that, while I was sleeping, God was watching over our baby. In that moment, I began praising Him for His faithfulness, love, and saving grace. I cannot even imagine what would've happened if I kept on sleeping

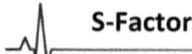

while Emily's fever got higher and she struggled to breathe all night.

My daughter is alive because God spoke to me. He woke me up from my slumber with a sense of urgency. He gave me divine directions in the midst of chaos. His still small voice is the reason why Emily is alive and a beacon of light today. I know my daughter is special, but my family is not unique. God speaks to each of us in different ways to save us from dangers seen and unseen.

He speaks to us through circumstances, other people, our thoughts, nature, and His Holy Word. I often say that God speaks to us through the wind, earthquakes or fire. The wind is a consistent voice that we hear everywhere we go, saying, "'This is the way, walk in it,' whenever you turn to the right hand or whenever you turn to the left" (Isaiah 30:21). The message is clear: turn away from sinful ways and seek the Lord with all our hearts.

**Bridgette Bastien**

Many of us have been hearing this consistent message for years. The wind, like God's Word, can be comforting on a cool day, but it can also blow us off our feet when we least expect it. We often ignore the wind when it's comforting, but we can't disregard it when it's a fierce force.

Like a strong wind, an earthquake often catches us off guard. Its sudden shocks and jolts send us running and hiding for cover and protection. I know this from my many years of living in Los Angeles. Earthquakes come in different magnitudes based on the Richter Scale. Most earthquakes below 4.5 will shake us, but the damage is minimal; however, earthquakes with magnitudes between five and ten will not only shake us, but will also cause severe damage and even death.

Like an earthquake below 4.5, God sometimes sends subtle spiritual shakes. These shakes are wakeup calls reminding us that "Jesus is coming soon" and urging us to "Make our calling and election sure." When we ignore these warnings, stronger spiritual earthquakes hit with more intensity. These more forceful and alarming messages declare, "Wake up! Time is running out!" or "Death is at the door" and they demand immediate action.

Strong wind and earthquakes are no match compared to fire. A fire is all consuming. It penetrates to the core and will engulf everything in its fury. In recent months, fires have destroyed thousands of acres in Australia, Brazil, Siberia, Oregon and California, taking the lives of many people and animals. Fire is destructive, but it can also be used for positive purposes. A goldsmith, for instance, uses fire to remove impurities from gold and other precious metals. Similarly, God uses the "refining fire" (Malachi 3: 2-3) to remove sin from our lives allowing us to submit to Him.

Once we submit, He is able to cleanse us from all unrighteousness. The refining process is never pleasant; however, it is necessary for us to reflect God's likeness and obey His voice when

**Bridgette Bastien**

He speaks to us. Elijah, a prominent prophet in the Old Testament, often heard God's voice. When was the last time you heard His voice?

It is remarkable to study how God spoke to Elijah during one of the most stressful times in his life. Elijah was running from Jezebel, the wicked queen of Israel, who intended to kill him. He became hopeless and questioned if he was the only faithful servant of God left in the world.

At this fragile point in Elijah's life, the Lord said to him, "Go forth, and stand upon the mount before the Lord. And, behold, the Lord passed by, and a great and strong wind rent the mountains, and brake in pieces the rocks before the Lord; but the Lord was not in the wind: and after the wind an earthquake; but the Lord was not in the earthquake: and after the earthquake a fire; but the Lord was not in the fire: and after the fire a still small voice" (1Kings 19:11-13)

God saw the anguish of Elijah's heart and wanted to grant him peace. God spoke directly

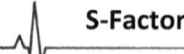

**S-Factor**

to Elijah, thereby strengthening his faith. He spoke in a still small voice forcing Elijah to listen attentively and to block out all the noises in his head. Are you running from a situation that seems bigger and stronger than you are? Stop and listen—God is speaking to you.

He speaks through the wind, earthquake, and fire. His message may come through a calm breeze, a jolting shake, or a consuming flame. Maybe He's speaking to you through this book. Can you hear Him? The message could be, "I am with you always even unto the end of the age" (Matthew 28:20); or "Believe on the Lord Jesus Christ, and you will be saved, you and your household" (Acts 16:31).

God doesn't need to shout. In fact, He usually whispers in a still small voice. If we heed His voice, we'll remain safe in the Lord's arms and maybe even help save someone's life. If we don't listen, we will be consumed by our sin. Our Savior speaks to each of us. We just have to listen and obey His voice when we hear it.

**Bridgette Bastien**

*Speak, Lord! Your servants are listening to You. We know You speak through different ways—through the wind, an earthquake, a fire, or Your still small voice. Help us to tune our ears and hearts to Your voice. We understand that obedience can make the difference between life and death. Your Word is life, and without it, we'd be hopeless. Thank you for continuing to speak to us and building our faith which comes from hearing, and hearing through the word of Christ (Romans 10:17).*

S-Factor

# *S-Factor 11: Seeking Sinners*

I can recall the day when God spoke to my family through a storm. Raindrops hit our car window like a beating drum introducing an African dance. As the clouds burst open and emptied themselves on

> *"How think ye? If a man have an hundred sheep, and one of them be gone astray, doth he not leave the ninety and nine, and goeth into the mountains, and seeketh that which is gone astray?"*
>
> *Matthew 18:12, KJV*

us, I smiled from ear to ear. The weather was going to change our plans, and I wasn't sad about it. My oldest daughter, on the other hand, cried, "Why is it raining?"

The heavy rain came out of nowhere. Within a few minutes, showers and dark clouds overpowered the sunny, summer day. As the rain streamed down the car windows, I announced to my daughters, "It's raining too hard. We'll

**Bridgette Bastien**

have to reschedule your playdate for another time." Though pleased with the change in weather, I was not quite ready for the storm that erupted in the car. They both whimpered and whined in despair. I smiled. I wanted nothing more than to go home and relax after work.

"Mommy, we don't want to go home! We promised our friends we'd have a playdate. Can you P-L-E-A-S-E just drive by the ice cream place to see if they're there?" Emily asked. I tried hard to block out their cries of distress.

"Mommy? Are you listening to us?" Elise asked.

"That makes no sense, it'll take us over 15 minutes to get there, and it's pouring outside," I said to the girls.

Emily replied, "Please mommy, please! While you drive there, I am going to pray to God and ask Him to stop the rain." I chuckled out loud while thinking, *'Yeah right! God is not going to*

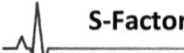 **S-Factor**

*stop the rain because you want to have a playdate.'*

I doubted her plan would work, but for my sanity, I drove toward the creamery for the playdate. Yes, in that moment, I questioned the power of prayer. (Actually, I hoped that God wouldn't answer her prayer and answer mine instead.) It appeared that God was on my side when we were about five minutes away from our destination.

The sky poured out everything it had on us. Lightning zapped back and forth across the black, ominous clouds. The rain hitting the windshield went from pitter-pattering drops to pounding sheets of water. The ferocious weather made me second-guess my decision to head toward the creamery. "I must be mad driving to a playdate in this storm," I said to the girls.

Emily simply responded, "I am praying, Mommy."

**Bridgette Bastien**

Less than two minutes away, the boisterous rain instantaneously stopped. The gray clouds skipped away like happy kids at a park. The storm calmed and the sun shined in all its glory. It was as if God said to the storm, "Peace be still" like He did in Mark 4:35-38. In jubilation, my daughters began screaming for joy as we pulled into the creamery's parking lot. Emily yelled, "God did it again! He answered my prayers! We can have our playdate now!"

Elise chimed in with "Go God! Go God! It's time for ice cream!" In disbelief, I parked the car and sat dumbfounded that God actually stopped the rain. The wet, shiny parking lot juxtaposed with the sunny skies told the whole story. I was honestly a bit annoyed, but the abrupt change in weather reminded me that God will go to any extent to seek His children, save us, and strengthen our faith.

Despite my wishes to go home, He answered my daughters' prayers. This gave them confidence in God's ability to hear and answer

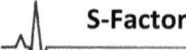 **S-Factor**

prayers. They couldn't wait to tell their friends about what God did for them. While we ate ice cream, they relived our drive to the creamery.

"Mommy is no fun. She wanted to go home, but we prayed to God. The rain started getting worse, but we kept on praying. Then, it stopped," Elise said. Emily interjected, "I knew God would answer our prayers." The girls were doing more talking than eating. Their experience with God was sweeter than ice cream could ever be. Are your interactions with God more satisfying than your favorite food?

God desires to build eternal relationships with His children. He'll do anything to save just one sinner. This is not only coming from a mother impressed with how God blessed her daughters, this is a biblical truth. The Bible asks, "How think ye? If a man has an hundred sheep, and one of them be gone astray, doth he not leave the ninety and nine, and goeth into the mountains, and seeketh that which is gone astray?" (Matthew 18:12, KJV) Would you consider leaving ninety-nine people to seek and save one lost soul? Some of us may not, but God does on a daily basis. I have witnessed and heard many testimonies about how far God goes to save one soul.

One of my most memorable salvation stories is about a young man, we'll call "Robbie." Robbie was born and raised in the church. He was tall, dark, and had a confident strut. His baby face was often overlooked because of his rugged voice. He came to church with his family almost every Wednesday night and Sabbath morning with his Bible tucked under his arm. He always had a warm smile. He dressed according to church norms and actively participated in Sabbath school. There was no reason to believe that he would ever become a lost sheep.

Robbie's transformation, or rebellion, as some church folk deemed it, happened within one year. In less than 365 days, his church attendance grew sporadic and he no longer showed interest in God's Word. Robbie, though once put together, now wore sagging pants and had uncombed hair. His change manifested itself not only in his sudden distaste for church, but also, in his attitude toward others. He became disrespectful, angry, and was quick to fight other kids.

Everyone was concerned about Robbie. Some church members focused on his attitude, while others viewed his new dress code as a negative reflection on the church. I did not agree with most of Robbie's actions, but I supported him and his family. I knew this young man was not acting out because he had a rebellious spirit; he was dealing with the devastation of his mom's chronic disease.

I knew his mother's medical ups and downs, their depleted bank account, and almost empty refrigerator, were taking a toll on him. He was a teenager dealing with grown folks' problems while being judged by those who should've been supporting him. Robbie finally

**Bridgette Bastien**

went over the edge when they lost their home and had to move in with family members.

He was crying out for help, but some church members were too busy casting judgements rather than recognizing his pain. To the glory of God, there were a few church members who rallied around Robbie and his family during their time of need. Like Robbie, today, there are many people crying out for help in our churches and communities. Can you hear them?

Robbie's cry for help and my daughters' persistent plea for sunshine remind me of Bartimaeus' story in Mark 10. Bartimaeus was blind from birth. He spent his days sitting by the street side covered in dirty, tattered clothes. With his arms stretched out gripping a small basket with a few coins, he pleaded with passersby to spare some change. He did this each day until the moment he met Jesus.

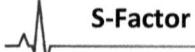 **S-Factor**

As Jesus was leaving Jericho, He passed by Bartimaeus who cried out and said, "Jesus, Son of David, have mercy on me!" Instead of helping or encouraging Bartimaeus, the people around him sternly told him to be quiet. They viewed his cry as a disruption to their peace. Are you listening to those who tell you to stay quiet, or are you earnestly pleading with God?

The crowd's annoyance would have silenced some people but Bartimaeus cried out even more. "Son of David, have mercy on me!" he exclaimed. His perseverance made the difference. In Mark 10:51, Jesus turned to him and said, "What do you want Me to do for you?" This simple question is powerful on many levels. It's a question that Jesus is asking us today. What is your greatest need?

Jesus asked this question not out of ignorance but because He wanted Bartimaeus to verbalize his needs. Bartimaeus replied, "Rabboni, that I may receive my sight." He could have asked for riches, houses or land, but his greatest need was the ability to see. Bartimaeus focused on the most important thing because he quickly discerned that this interaction with Jesus was a chance of a lifetime.

Like Bartimaeus, our priorities need to be in order. When we go to Jesus, we should pray that our will aligns to His. More often than not, we are asking God to line our pockets with silver and gold. Christ is able to do that and so much more so why not ask for something priceless. Jesus answered Bartimaeus with, "Go your way; your faith has made you well" (verse 52). Do you believe your faith can make you whole?

Jesus didn't judge Bartimaeus like some church members judged Robbie. Jesus didn't ignore him like I tried to ignore my daughters. Jesus always focuses on the lost and those in need of His help. The Bible says, "There will be more joy in heaven over one sinner who repents than over ninety-nine just persons who need no repentance" (Luke 15:7). Many churches are fixed on the ninety-nine who appear "saved,"

S-Factor

but lose sight of the one who has strayed away. Jesus, the seeker of sinners, never loses sight of those who are lost.

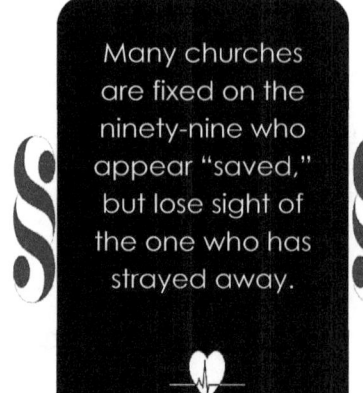
Many churches are fixed on the ninety-nine who appear "saved," but lose sight of the one who has strayed away.

This is very reassuring, for we are all sinners who need repentance. Some of us wear our sins like a warm, fitted coat on a wintery night. Some of us mistakenly flaunt them thinking that there are "big sins" and "small sins." We are not called to flaunt or hide our sins, but rather to acknowledge them, repent, and ask God for forgiveness. God says, "For My eyes are on all their ways; they are not hidden from My face, nor is their iniquity hidden from My eyes" (Jeremiah 16:17). God knows everything about us. He wants nothing more than for us to repent and stay within the safety of His love.

Just like Robbie, we're all susceptible to going astray. If we were lost, we would want someone to come looking for us. This is why Jesus leaves the ninety-nine and goes looking for the lost one. Following Christ's example, we are called to seek the lost. William A. Ogden, author and musician, wrote the song, "Seeking the Lost." The second verse says,

> *Seeking the lost and pointing to Jesus*
> *Souls that are weak and hearts that are sore*
> *Leading them forth in ways of salvation*
> *Showing the path to life evermore.*

Our role, as children of God, is to prayerfully search for those wandering away and point them back to Jesus. We can do this in many ways—offer words of encouragement, meet their physical needs, and/or intercede for them consistently when we pray. I continue to pray that Robbie finds his way back to the Lord. He has been through so much, but I'm confident that all of his tests will one day become a part of his powerful testimony.

If you feel lost, like Robbie, know that the Lord hears your prayer. You're not alone and someone cares. If you are running away from

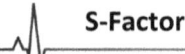 **S-Factor**

God because you don't feel worthy of His love, make a decision at this moment to stop and turn to Him. Jesus doesn't care what you wore last night, what you said last week, where you were last month, or what you did last year. Jesus' only desire is to seek and save sinners. Once we are saved, we too must lovingly seek sinners, lead them to Jesus, and help strengthen their faith.

 *God, You sought us when we weren't even thinking about You. You sacrificed Your Son, even while we were still sinners. You answer whenever we call and reassure us during times of uncertainty. You're a miracle worker. You have the power to calm any storm, and a deep love for the lost. We want to be as compassionate to others as You have been to us. We want to seek after You like you sought after us. Save us, Lord!*

**Bridgette Bastien**

# S-Factor 12: Sincerely Saved

Seeking sinners and transforming them into earthly saints is the purpose of Jesus. Emily indeed looked like a saint dressed in her off-

> *"Let the redeemed of the Lord say so, whom He has redeemed from the hand of the enemy."*
>
> Psalms 107:2

white, gem studded, chiffon dress, with its pink, satin bow. Her off-white barrettes peeked around her regal bun which sat like a crown on her head. Emily's eyes sparkled like diamonds while her contagious smile and calm spirit revealed nothing but peace.

Unlike her, I was a nervous wreck. I couldn't stop jittering and squeezing the palms of my hands in anticipation. It was one of the happiest days of my life, but my nerves were getting the best of me. I was witnessing my oldest daughter's baptism at our church and I wanted everything

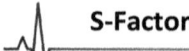 **S-Factor**

to be perfect. It was indeed memorable, not only for my family, but also for two other families.

As I looked around the church, the members of each family were beaming with joy and expectation. The congregation was watching God's love manifested in the lives of three individuals on that day—each of them from diverse backgrounds and with different stories. Though their stories were different, there was one common thread woven through each story—prayer saves lives!

At nine years old, Emily decided to be baptized. She demanded that the adults in her life take her seriously. While her father and I always prayed for our children to be saved, we never anticipated that she would commit her life to God at such an early age. We had no intentions of stopping her, but we wanted to make sure she understood the magnitude of her decision.

**Bridgette Bastien**

She repeatedly told us that she was sure and absolutely wanted to "give her life to Jesus." After several months of Bible studies and working with the pastor and elders, everyone felt Emily was ready for baptism. She was bursting with excitement and smiling from ear to ear on the day of her baptism. Her reaction reminded me of the Ethiopian eunuch.

After the eunuch's brief interaction and Bible study session with the disciple Philip, he asked, "See, here is water. What hinders me from being baptized?" (Acts 8:36). The eunuch didn't hesitate to surrender his life to God. He didn't need to hear 10,000 sermons before deciding to get baptized. He didn't even ponder the possibilities of losing friends once he met the ultimate friend, Jesus.

He eagerly urged Philip to baptize him, and afterwards the Bible says, "He [the eunuch] went on his way rejoicing" (Acts 8:39). He went away happy and looking forward to sharing God's love with others. Have you been

## S-Factor

contemplating baptism or are you already baptized and trying to find ways to share Christ with others? Pray and ask God for guidance as you dedicate your life to do His will.

On the day of Emily's baptism, eight-year-old Danny was dedicated to God by his parents. Danny was usually very active and talkative. He was often the first child to raise his hand to answer questions during Sabbath school. Whether or not he knew the right answer, he was eager to share what he knew with his classmates. Sometimes, he would also gaze off into the distance, as if lost in another world.

When you finally got his attention, he would happily explain what was happening in his imagination. This was Danny on a typical day—full of passion and zeal. But during his dedication, he stood quietly in his sharp navy-blue suit and white shirt as he listened to the words being spoken over his life by the pastor. His calm disposition revealed God's peace within him, which put a big smile on my face.

**Bridgette Bastien**

As I witnessed Danny's dedication, I reflected on Hannah's story in 1 Samuel chapter one. Hannah was married to Elkanah, but remained barren after years of trying to conceive a child. She faithfully prayed for a son. She prayed daily while being ridiculed by her husband's other wife. Her rival doubted that she would ever have a child. Even the priest, Eli, questioned what she was doing in the temple as she "prayed to the Lord and wept in anguish" (verse 10).

Despite the naysayers, Hannah persevered in prayer and her dream became a reality. When God answered Hannah's prayers and opened her womb, she didn't forget her promise to Him. Have you ever reneged on your pledge to God? Many times, we make promises to God in the midst of our trials and tribulations, but we forget them or intentionally break those vows after He delivers us.

Hannah followed through on her pledge and demonstrated her gratitude in an admirable

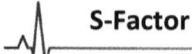 S-Factor

way. Hannah said to Eli the priest, "I am the woman who stood by you here, praying to the Lord. For this child I prayed, and the Lord has granted me my petition which I asked of Him. Therefore, I also have lent him to the Lord; as long as he lives, he shall be lent to the Lord" (I Samuel 1: 26-28). Hannah did not hesitate to return back to God the gift He had given her. Her sacrifice was tremendous.

Like Hannah, Danny's parents willingly returned their son to the Lord. They were not deterred by society's norm of dedicating a child prior to their second birthday. They believed it's never too late to give a child back to God. This is a great example for parents today who are struggling with their children—regardless of age. It's also never too late for us, as parents or adults, to repent and return to God.

Jerry learned this lesson after years of running away from God. Jerry was a pastor's son, born and raised in the church. As a youth, he was a leader and very active in his church community. In his early 20s, he left home and deserted his family because he felt restricted by their rules. He was on a mission to explore the world—to do everything and try anything his heart desired, without restriction.

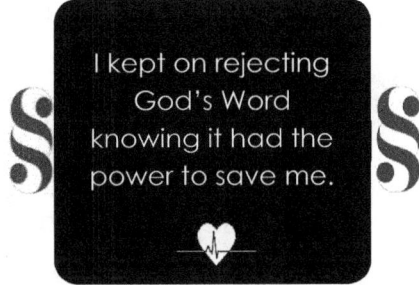

"I was constantly searching for love in all the wrong places, which lead to a life of homosexuality," Jerry said to the church. His eyes scanned the room effortlessly as he shared his story after the baptism and dedication service. Many in the church were on the edge of their pews as we listened to his captivating and tear-jerking testimony.

"My happiness was temporary and even after partying, I was left lonely, empty and sad. I kept on rejecting God's Word knowing it had the power to save me," he recalled. As Jerry told his chronicles, I could picture the emotional turmoil he experienced over the past twenty years. His

 **S-Factor**

testimony was raw and his transformation was radical.

Now in his forties, standing there in his neatly pressed shirt and dark slacks, he stated, "I didn't have the strength to pray for myself over the years, but I knew my parents and sister were praying for me." Jerry's family prayed for him for over twenty years, even when he wanted nothing to do with God. Their faith helped pull him out of darkness and push him back into the Lord's arms. He eventually confessed his sins, cried out to Jesus for help, and decided to give his life to the Lord.

Jerry's journey emphasizes the importance of repentance and epitomizes God's amazing grace. Like Jerry, Zacchaeus also reaped the benefits of mercy and grace as highlighted in Luke 19. Zacchaeus is known for being vertically challenged and climbing a tree to see Jesus. We often focus on Zacchaeus being in the sycamore tree, but miss the real story.

**Bridgette Bastien**

Zacchaeus was born and raised in the church. He most likely knew the truth as a young Jewish boy, but strayed from God as he got older. Zacchaeus got enticed by worldly pleasures—wealth, property, and material goods. He even used his job, as tax collector, to defraud others which made him a traitor in the eyes of his own people.

Although others rejected him, Jesus said to him, "Zacchaeus, make haste and come down, for today I must stay at your house" (Luke 19:5). This wasn't just Jesus inviting Himself over for dinner. These words restored Zacchaeus, who was acutely aware of his need for a Savior. It was also a lesson in love for many in the crowd who despised Zacchaeus. After willingly confessing his sins and repenting, Zacchaeus surrendered his life to God.

Jesus confirmed this by saying, "Today salvation has come to this house, because he also is a son of Abraham; for the Son of Man has come to seek and to save that which was lost"

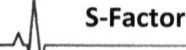 S-Factor

(Luke 19:9, 10). Although he initially departed from the faith like Jerry, Zacchaeus eventually chose to accept the free gift of salvation.

There is nothing like choosing to be a part of God's family. God chose us before we were born. We must decide whether or not we will accept and unwrap His gift. My daughter, Emily, made the decision herself and boldly walks in God's grace. Led by his parents, Danny calmly embraced the gift of God. The prayers and love of Jerry's family snatched him back from hopelessness, and God's forgiveness saved him.

The power of prayer truly saved these three souls. Are you saved? If yes, continue to serve God with your whole heart. If not, open your heart today and pray that God will come in and stay forever. If you can't find the right words now, you can repeat these words in faith:

> *Dear God, I come to You in Jesus' name. I acknowledge that I'm a sinner. I have not always obeyed or honor You, but I repent*

*of my sins. I believe that Christ died for me, was buried and rose from the dead. I believe that Christ is the only way to salvation. Come into my heart Jesus, I want You as my personal Lord and Savior.*

Once you've said these words, believe you're saved and start living according to God's Word.

*Thank you, Lord for the plan of Salvation. It's a wonderful thing not only when we give our lives over to you, but also when we witness others doing the same. Salvation is a gift for sinners—a gift that keeps on giving. Some of us come to You willingly after experiencing Your love and others are pushed into Your arms by the pressures of life. Regardless of our path, thank you for meeting us where we are. You're the most gracious and sacrificial gift-giver.*

## S-Factor 13: Salvation in Sychar

Being sincerely saved is better than enjoying any fancy meal. This is coming from "a certified foodie." Food has always played an integral part in my life.

> "Therefore also now, saith the Lord, turn ye even to me with all your heart, and with fasting, and with weeping, and with mourning"
>
> Joel 2:12, KJV

The flavor of cornmeal porridge sweetened with condensed milk, accented with cinnamon, nutmeg, and vanilla awakens possibilities each morning.

The color of ackee and saltfish sprinkled with green scallions, bright red tomatoes, and pale-yellow onions brightens the darkest days. The savory smell of soup packed with yellow yam, boiled dumplings, pumpkin, and carrots comforts my soul—especially on a rainy day. Yes, I love food.

**Bridgette Bastien**

Being a "foodie," I've often struggled with fasting. I try to fast as often as possible, but it can be a challenge. I know I'm not alone as most people believe that they can't go without food for a few hours, much less a day. Food is considered the sustainer of life. Whenever there is an opportunity to fast, even Christians are reluctant. Some people hesitate, or even refuse, to fast in anticipation of stomach pains, headaches, dizziness, and grumpiness.

The reality is fasting requires sacrifice, and the physical repercussions are not always pleasant. For these reasons, I wasn't too happy after being reminded to fast during an early morning prayer session. I said in my heart, *I don't think so*. I made the decision not to fast soon after hanging up the phone. I didn't want to go through the physical discomfort while having to work a full day. I was content with my decision until the next morning.

During my devotions, I read in Hebrews 5:9: "He [Christ] became the author of eternal salvation to all who obey Him." Convicted in my heart, I got on my knees and prayed for strength to obey God. I never anticipated how the decision to fast would change my day, and I had no clue that my obedience would impact the lives of others.

On the way to work, I had the urge to call one of my former church sisters, Jackie, who lived in a different state. I also had the urge to stop and get breakfast at a local restaurant. Instead of grabbing food, I dialed Jackie's number expecting to get her voicemail because she was usually at work during that time. Jackie picked up the phone with a solemn hello, but as soon as she heard my voice, she started praising God.

"Thank you, Jesus! Lord, You are awesome, faithful, and kind," she said. Jackie had been depressed for several weeks. Due to the death of a family member, she struggled to make it through each day, but prayed for God to send someone to encourage her. She shared how she had just finished praying about needing someone to talk to. "God has consistently sent people from my past to uplift me and today He sent you," she commented. We both started praising God for His wonderful works.

As we talked, I opened up about God's faithfulness toward me. I shared how by God's grace, I escaped from a serious car accident without any broken bones even though my car was totaled.[5] I admitted that God placed a hedge around me to ensure that as "I walk through the valley of the shadow of death, I will fear no evil" (Psalms 23:4, KJV).

We both continued testifying, praising, and worshipping God. Our spirits were lifted and I felt like I was floating on air. Our conversation turned into almost an hour of reflecting, adoring, and proclaiming that "there's no God like Jehovah." All in the same conversation, we talked, laughed, cried, sang, shouted, and at moments, quietly

---

[5] My first book, OVERCOMER, captures this testimony in its entirety. Book available at www.prayersavedmylife.com/books

reflected on God's goodness. Have you ever had such an experience?

After saying our goodbyes, I walked into my office, ready to take on the world. I didn't realize this was just the beginning of the fullness I would experience through fasting. I had several bouts of hunger pains during the morning but prayed through them and meditated on scriptures like Daniel 9:3 and Ezra 8:23. Both of these verses reinforce the importance of fasting and praying.

Three hours later, one of my mentees, Annabelle, stopped by my office. I thought it was going to be an upbeat conversation until she said, "I've been in and out of the hospital for the past few weeks." I wrongly guessed that she had the flu. She looked at me and said, "It's much worse." Annabelle admitted that she was suffering from depression and had often contemplated suicide. She then whispered, "Everyone in my immediate family is clinically

**Bridgette Bastien**

depressed, and I've already lost two family members to suicide."

As she spoke, my heart dropped and my desire for food faded away. Annabelle recalled intimate details of her life and her family's mental health history. Their struggle with mental health went back many generations and included some fatalities. I didn't know what to do or say, but as I opened my mouth several encouraging words from God came rushing from my lips.

I shared scriptures like "Cast all your care upon Him, for He cares for you" (1 Peter 5:7), "When the righteous cry for help the Lord hears and delivers them out of all their troubles" (Psalms 34:17) and You are "fearfully and wonderfully made" (Psalms 139:14). I felt myself being emptied as we talked, and I witnessed her posture changing during our conversation.

Annabelle's low-hanging head was now lifted high. Her shoulders were no longer drooping. Her tears slowly dried up and a smile took over her face. She went through a drastic transformation within thirty minutes time. Before we parted ways, Annabelle admitted being uncomfortable with telling her story due to fear of criticism. She expressed how grateful she was that I listened without judging her.

"Thank you, Bridgette. It's rare to find someone I can open up to. Each time we talk, you always make me feel better. Today, you really allowed God to use you," she said. We often interact with people, but we rarely know their story. I held her hands and prayed that God would give her peace and remind her every day that life was worth living. She walked out of my office smiling.

Later in the evening, while reflecting on my day, a scripture came to mind: "But do not forget to do good and to share, for with such sacrifices God is well pleased" (Hebrews 13:16). I realized why God wanted me to fast. It wasn't just about restraining from food. It was about obedience and being available for Him to use me. Instead of eating, or thinking about the meals I was missing, I stayed focused on God.

If I hadn't surrendered to Him and decided to fast, I may not have been there for these women in their moments of need. Because of my sacrifice, God was able to use me to bless His daughters. When I think about sacrifice, I think about Jesus. He was always willing to give up food in order to follow the Holy Spirit and do the will of His Father.

Jesus even confessed, "My food is to do the will of Him who sent me and to finish His work" (John 4:34, KJV). He uttered these words to His disciples after an interesting encounter with a Samaritan woman. Jesus and His disciples were travelling from Judea to Galilee. The direct route is some 70 miles, but most Jews avoided this route and went the long way around Samaria so they wouldn't have any dealings with the Samaritan people. Jesus decided to go directly through Samaria because he had a divine appointment.

**S-Factor**

Once they got to the town of Sychar, He sent His disciples away for two reasons: to get food and to make sure that no one interfered with His ministry. Sometimes we have to dismiss our distractions and separate from our cliques to do ministry.

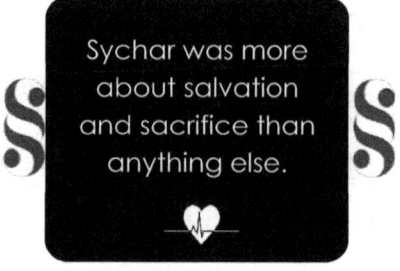
Sychar was more about salvation and sacrifice than anything else.

Jesus patiently waited for the Samaritan woman at Jacob's well. He engaged the woman in a conversation by asking her for a drink of water. They discussed "living water," "having multiple husbands," and "true, spiritual worship." Their conversation, as recorded in John 4: 9-15, was life-changing. On the surface, the dialogue appears to be about a promiscuous woman coming to grips with her lifestyle. Looking deeper, it was about accepting the gift of eternal life that Jesus offered the Samaritan woman and her entire village.

Jesus offers each of us the same gift and reveals that Sychar was more about salvation and sacrifice than anything else. In this small town where Jacob's well provided physical water, Christ offered the Samaritans living water. This living water would not only quench their thirst, but would also break down gender and generational barriers. Once these barriers were broken, a disreputable woman became an evangelist and the Samaritans transitioned from being irrelevant to becoming important.

The Samaritans, whom the Jews considered second-class citizens, were given first-class treatment by Jesus. Sychar was indeed about salvation. The Samaritan woman gave up her pride, faced her tainted past, and confessed her secret sins to Jesus. Salvation is impossible without sacrifice. The Samaritan woman gave up her sinful ways and Jesus willingly went without physical food until each soul in Sychar was converted to God.

Jesus' sacrifice saved Sychar. The villagers proclaimed to the Samaritan woman, "Now we believe, not because of what you said, for we ourselves have heard Him and we know that this is indeed the Christ, the Savior of the world" (John 4:42). Imagine the transformation in our communities, and the impact on the world, if we brought everyone, we know to meet Jesus.

Envision the difference in our families if we fasted like Jesus and experienced the power that comes from being filled with the Holy Spirit. Consider the possibilities if we stop trying to overcome spiritual giants in our own way, but instead, remember that "this kind does not go out except by prayer and fasting" (Matthew 17:21). Many more people can be saved and freed from spiritual shackles if we allow God to equip us and use us as He sees fit.

Sacrifice in Sychar is not just about staying away from physical food or going through hunger pains until the next meal. Isaiah 58:6, 7 reminds us that an acceptable fast is "to loose the bonds of wickedness, to undo the heavy burdens, to let the oppressed go free, and [to] break every yoke...to share your bread with the

**Bridgette Bastien**

hungry, and...bring to your house the poor who are cast out, [and] when you see the naked, that you cover him." Sacrifice in Sychar is about surrendering to God. If we yield, God will redeem our lives and the lives of everyone we encounter. Then, even foodies like me will eagerly fast to overcome sinful desires, bless others, and experience God's fullness.

The next time there's an opportunity to fast, let's consider the spiritual and eternal benefits rather than the temporary and physical discomfort. The flavor, color, and smell of food are exquisite, but turning from sin and giving our hearts to God are divine. Cornmeal porridge with condensed milk is sweet, but even sweeter is the joy of a new Christian. Soup is deliciously savory, but not more than the testimony of someone who has been saved by God's grace.

By sacrificing something, each of us can make a difference in someone's life. Christ sacrificed His life on Calvary's cross—surely one person having the opportunity to accept the free

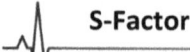 **S-Factor**

gift of salvation is worth us giving up a plate, or two, of food. What are you willing to sacrifice in order for your loved ones to accept and unwrap the gift salvation?

*Thank you, Lord. Your sacrifice secured salvation for us. Although we sometimes hesitate to sacrifice, we understand that You may call upon us to give up something in order to bless someone. We know that many people are hurting in silence. Open our eyes and soften our hearts so we can recognize and comfort those in pain. Fasting can be physically painful but missing the chance to tell others about You is more detrimental. Just like we hunger and thirst for food, help us to crave You and Your Word.*

**Bridgette Bastien**

# *S-Factor 14: Simple "?"*

Sychar is about reflecting on how far we've come and looking ahead to a brighter future. I recently had a

> "For what if some did not believe? Will their unbelief make the faithfulness of God without effect?"
>
> Romans 3:3

moment of reflection while meandering through the crowded Boston Convention Center. I never anticipated I would be thrust down memory lane when I first signed up for the conference.

After listening to several phenomenal women share their stories, my colleague—we'll call her, Susanne—and I decided to check out the vendors' booths. We stopped at the booth of a major pharmaceutical company and chatted with the representative for a few minutes. After walking away, Susanne said, "I can't believe you used to work for them as a chemist." She peppered me with career questions then paused and looked at me before asking, "What made you stick with chemistry? It's such a difficult subject."

I smiled and began sharing my high school and college journey. "I had a great science teacher in high school who made the subject come alive," I said. "It didn't seem difficult to me then. In fact, it was fun, especially the chemistry laboratories." Susanne attentively listened to my story. I paused awhile before saying, "College was a bit different. Yes, the subject became more advanced, but the most difficult part was not having the support of my first advisor, who was also Head of the Chemistry Department."

I recalled when he told me that "People like me don't major in chemistry." The comment, "People like me," could've either meant people of African descent or women in general. I never questioned him about his racist or sexist comment. I knew right away it was meant to deter me from achieving my academic goals. Instead of confronting him, I called my mother crying hysterically and told her I was going to quit chemistry. I expected her to cuddle me over the phone with sweet words as I bared my soul.

My mom responded, "Don't let anyone define you based on their preconceived notions. Tomorrow, I want you to change advisors. If you don't call me by early afternoon and tell me you have a new advisor, I am coming up to your college." My mother was not bluffing. She was ready to deal with the doubters who were hindering my academic progress. Susanne began laughing and then asked, "Your mom was planning to pop up at your college?"

"My advisor had power and influence on campus, but an angry Jamaican mother was not to be played with," I responded. "I was more scared of my mom than my advisor." I did exactly as my mother demanded, and by 3 p.m. the following day, and by the grace of God, I had a new advisor. After this, I was even more determined to become a successful scientist and to prove my doubters wrong.

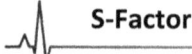 **S-Factor**

Susanne, fully engaged in my life's journey, then asked, "What if your mother never stepped in and encouraged you?" I shrugged my shoulders indicating that I had no idea what would've happened to my chemistry career without her intervention. My mother's love and a new advisor's support helped propel me to have a prosperous academic and professional career in chemistry.

I told Susanne that a couple of years later, my original advisor—the one who wanted to crush my career dreams—requested that I speak to incoming students. He wanted me to talk about the great things that were happening in the Chemistry department. Supposedly, he was proud of my accomplishments and how I represented the college during my summer internship at a major pharmaceutical company.

I thought twice about making that speech because of who the request came from, but eventually did it to honor those who supported me through the tough times. After college, I had many fruitful years working for three top pharmaceutical companies. I wouldn't have gotten that far without my mom's love and support.

As I drove home later that evening from the conference, Susanne's simple question stuck with me. The question of "What if...?" evoked both joyful and painful emotions as I strolled down memory lane. The answer to such a question is never straightforward. "What if" challenges us to consider the possibilities and ramifications before we make certain decisions or take certain actions in life.

"What if" is like a fork in the road pointing in different directions on our journey; it's like binoculars staring into the future despite an uncertain present. "What if" can also be a rearview mirror magnifying our past as we reflect on how our choices got us to where we are today. Whether we're looking forward or backward in time, any decision without divine guidance will be detrimental to our lives.

## S-Factor

On the other hand, decisions made with divine counsel lead to unlimited potential, peace, and prosperity. Have you ever pondered the "what ifs" of life? What if God never created man? Just imagine for a moment if God, through His infinite wisdom, knowing how sin would destroy the world, decided not to create us. The creation account in Genesis 1 would read very differently.

God would've said, "Let there be light. Let us separate waters from waters. Let the water be gathered to one place, let dry ground appear, and the land produce vegetation. Let there be a sun to rule the day, a moon to rule the night, and let stars appear. Let the water be filled with fish, and let birds fly in the sky. Finally, let the land produce animals." What if God stopped there?

He didn't because of His infinite love for mankind. God created us despite our unfaithfulness and disobedience. He then saved us through the obedience and sacrifice of Jesus Christ. Thinking about obedience to God, another question comes to mind: What if Adam and Eve never perverted God's command? What if they never ate from the Tree of Good and Evil in the middle of the garden? (See Genesis 2:16, 17)

Adam and Eve's defiance had immediate ramifications for them—harsh consequences which are still impacting humankind today. If they had obeyed God, we would be living in the Garden of Eden enjoying all the benefits of a sinless life and experiencing an intimate, unobstructed relationship with the Creator. Just like Adam and Eve, we often lose out on closeness with God because of disobedience.

Sin broke their bond with God. Sin is the reason for centuries of chaos. It's the reason for all the "isms" in our world, including racism, sexism, and classism, that we struggle with daily. Just imagine, ten generations after Adam and Eve, the world was filled with so much sin that God said, "I will destroy man whom I have created from the face of the earth…for I am sorry that I have made them" (Genesis 6:7). Destroying the earth was the only solution, and this grieved the Lord.

What if Noah didn't believe God when He said that a flood would destroy the world? It may seem obvious to us because we've experienced rain and the devastating impact of various hurricanes. But if we had never seen rain before, the concept of a flood would have been inconceivable. It took great faith for Noah and his family to believe God. If Noah hadn't trusted God, or had lost faith years before the flood, his entire family would have perished—all humanity would have ceased to exist. We often don't realize it, but our faith, or lack thereof, can make the difference in someone else's salvation.

What if at Calvary, Jesus said, "No, I will not sacrifice myself for this sinful human race?" The very people Jesus came to save denied Him, wrongly accused Him, as well as beat and spat on Him. They forgot all the miracles He performed as they yelled, "Crucify Him, crucify Him!" (Luke

23:21). He was forced to carry His own cross for miles as blood gushed from His head because of the 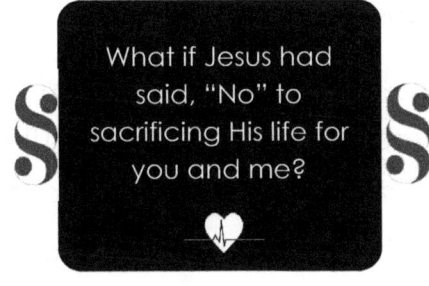 crown of thorns pressed into His skull.

Close your eyes and try to catch a glimpse of the "Giver of Life" becoming lifeless as He made His way to Calvary. He was so weak that the Roman soldiers forced Simon of Cyrene to help carry Jesus' cross. He was later nailed to the same cross and crucified, "yet He opened not his mouth" (Isaiah 53:7, KJV). While those He came to save disrespected and rejected Him, He remained quiet.

Jesus had more than enough reasons to reject the plan of salvation. He even went through Hematidrosis while praying in the Garden of Gethsemane. What if Jesus had said, "No" to sacrificing His life for you and me? We should all be grateful that Jesus said, "Yes." His decision to go all the way to Calvary is the reason, "every knee will bow, of those in heaven and of those on earth, and of those under the earth, and that every tongue should confess that Jesus Christ is Lord, to the glory of God the Father" (Philippians 2:10, 11). His gift—His sacrifice—made it possible for each of us to have eternal life.

The concept of eternal life may be difficult for some people to grasp. Many don't believe in the soon return of our Savior, Jesus Christ. This is evident based on how we treat each other and how we live each day. We step over the homeless or cross the street so we aren't bothered by them. We shut our car doors and roll up our windows as panhandlers approach our cars. We live in excess and throw away food while many are hungry in our neighborhoods.

Although we are living as if Jesus' coming is not near, the signs of the times (wars, rumors of wars, earthquakes in divers' places, COVID-19, human trafficking, child slavery, and many more) prove otherwise. Are you overlooking these signs or taking them seriously? Whenever I watch the news or read my social media feed, I am convinced that Christ's return is inevitable and closer than we believe.

Christians, no matter how old we are, have always heard that Jesus is coming soon. The Bible says that no one except God knows the day or the hour that Jesus is coming. In that day, two people will be together and only one of them will be taken away to be with Jesus, leaving the other behind (Matthew 24:35-42). These words should trigger a sense of urgency in each of us. We can't wait until the last minute because none of us knows when it will be. We must be ready. We must be earnest in expectation.

We have a choice to make each day. The choice to believe God or not. It's a personal choice. Consider this: what if every word, verse, chapter, and book in the Bible is true? Despite what some people believe, what if the Bible is not just fictional stories made up to entertain us? What if doubting and rejecting even one portion of God's Word means we are sealing our fate for

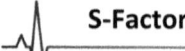 **S-Factor**

eternity? What if we don't prepare and the day, or hour, comes upon us like a thief in the night? What if Jesus returns and we're eternally lost because we've decided not to serve God with all of our hearts?

The answers to these questions are not simple. They are not insignificant. They should force us to evaluate, and re-evaluate, our salvation. Whether we've suffered setbacks or surpassed expectations, severed friendships or strived in relationships, stressed about money or succeeded financially, struggled with our faith or fully surrendered to God—salvation is the most important factor in this life.

Each of us should accept Christ's free gift of salvation. If we don't, we can't hold anyone else accountable for that decision. The opinion of doubters in our past shouldn't deter us. Our mother's love, no matter how comforting, cannot save us. We are sinners saved only by the sacrifice of a loving Savior—Jesus Christ.

Lord Jesus, life is not simple, but salvation is. You've asked us to believe and obey. Sometimes it's a struggle to have faith when we get distracted and temptations lead us away from You. We can hear You asking us this simple question, "Will you accept My gift of salvation today, unwrap it, and enjoy the benefits?" We answer, "YES," to Your will and way. Thank you, Lord, for saving us and giving us the choice to choose between life and death. We choose life; we choose You.

# Closing Thoughts: Salvation Is...

**Salvation is FREE!** I've intentionally mentioned it several times throughout this book. God crafted the plan of salvation before the existence of mankind. Jesus didn't ask us for anything before He voluntarily gave up His life on the cross at Calvary. We didn't have to surrender anything or suffer on a cross. No matter what some theologians or religious leaders may want us to believe, salvation is a free gift.

We don't deserve it, but God wants us to accept it. We may struggle with the notion that "salvation is free" because of common sayings like, "Nothing in life is free." Furthermore, we often give gifts with the intentions, or hope, that in the future, the favor will be reciprocated to us. This may be true when we are dealing with each other, but it's not true when we interact with God. His love and gift of salvation are free with no strings attached to them.

**Bridgette Bastien**

One of my favorite artists sang these words, *"The best things in life are free. Now, that I've discovered what you mean to me, the best things in life are free."* God created us because we mean the world to Him. Jesus then sacrificed everything, therefore paying the full price, to save us. He secured our salvation and freely offers eternal life to those willing to accept it.

Have you accepted His gift yet? Before I accepted Christ's gift of salvation, God tugged on my heart for years. When I was younger, I ignored Him and mistakenly thought the world had more to offer. I now know that temporary happiness can never compare to permanent joy. I also naively tried to pay my way into God's heart by doing "good deeds," but salvation is priceless. All the benevolence and riches in the world can never buy it. God freely gives agape love – a love strong enough to save sinners like you and me.

**Salvation is HARDWORK!** Just to be clear, we don't have to work for God to save us. He

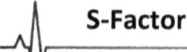 **S-Factor**

does it willingly, but once we accept His gift, we must unwrap it and begin to work. This work involves a lot of self-examination and daily surrendering of our desires and dreams to God's will. This work is not easy, but it is absolutely necessary.

The Bible story of Noah and the flood highlights this fact. God didn't require Noah to toil before He laid out the plan to save his family. God made the plan first, and after Noah's family accepted it, they became co-laborers with Him. They labored with God by preaching His Word and building the ark, despite years of ridicule and scoffing from others.

If it hasn't happened yet, there will come a day when we will have to defend our faith, in obedience to God, while others mock us. This is no simple task. It will be hardwork! After the flood, Noah's family continued to work. They cared for every mammal, bird, and reptile on the ark. Once we are saved, God expects us to care for everyone in our sphere of influence.

Those around us may act like lions or lambs, eagles or doves, snakes or snails, killer whales or goldfish. Their characters' strengths or flaws are irrelevant once God has empowered us to minister to them. They may even look different from us, require special treatment, and constantly test our patience, but once we are saved, we are called to serve.

**Salvation is a JOURNEY!** Each of us must decide whether or not we accept that "Christ is the Way, the Truth and the Life." Once we believe, the adventure begins. Sometimes our journey is filled with roses, but more often than not, it's overladen with thorns. Regardless of the path, we can't pack our s-factors—sins and sinful desires that separate us from God—and take them on this trip.

Sin will never take us where we want to go. It'll only cause us to spiral out of control. Like the Israelites, we have to leave Egypt behind, including all the things and people that once enslaved us. We need to focus on moving

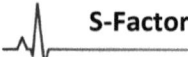 **S-Factor**

forward and making our way toward the Promised Land. What, or who, has kept you from moving forward in Christ?

The Israelites left Egypt and wandered through the wilderness for 40 years instead of 40 days. Their journey was long and traumatic because they clinged to their s-factors rather than God's hands. God protected and provided for the Israelites throughout their entire journey. He will do the same for us. He will be a cloud during the day and pillar of fire at night.

I equate "day" to when things are going well in life and "night" to when everything seems to be falling apart. Regardless of the time, God never leaves us. We may not be able to discern His presence, but He is always with us. He will also part the Red Sea, or troubled waters, in our lives to ensure we can safely cross it. He will then use the same body of water to destroy our enemies.

He will give us manna, angel food tasting like wafers made with honey when we're hungry, and water from a rock when we're thirsty. Once we hold onto God's hands, we will journey through life and eventually make it to the place God has in store for us—the heavenly Canaan, a land flowing with "milk and honey."

**Salvation is SWEET!** Without a doubt, each of us should be able to say, "I have tasted and seen that the Lord is good" (Psalm 34:8). We shouldn't only serve God because of how sweet salvation is or because of the things He has done for us. We should serve Him because He is worthy. He is the Creator. He is the Alpha and Omega. He is the Everlasting Father. Who is Jesus to you?

- If we acknowledge Him as our Savior, share the good news with someone. Let them know that, "The time is fulfilled, and the kingdom of God is at hand. Repent, and believe in the gospel" (Mark 1:15).
- If we've once walked with God, but now doubt Him, meditate on these words, "'Return, backsliding Israel,' says

the Lord; 'I will not cause My anger to fall on you. For I am merciful,' says the Lord; 'I will not remain angry forever'" (Jeremiah 3:12).

- If we've never had an intimate relationship with Jesus and we're more focused on worldly gains consider this scripture, "For what will it profit a man if he gains the whole world, and loses his own soul? Or what will a man give in exchange for his soul?" (Mark 8:36, 37).

For me, Salvation is as sweet as a big scoop of rocky-road ice cream topped with sprinkles, strawberries and chocolate syrup. The rocky road highlights our setbacks, severed friendships, and struggles. The sprinkles represent the diverse family of believers that we have the privilege to join once we accept His gift of salvation.

The strawberries are the delicious blessings that God continues to pour into our lives, even when we least expect it. The chocolate syrup is the overflow of love we've received and are called to give to others because we are followers of Christ. How would you describe your walk with God?

***Salvation is...!*** Fill in the blank based on your encounters with God. Regardless of our experiences, if we've had a free ride or paid the ultimate price, if we've worked hard or hardly worked, if we've journeyed for 40 days or 40 years, if we've enjoyed life's sweet syrups or bitter berries, we should be confident in this one thing: Jesus is our Savior.

We should willingly surrender every sin to Him and accept His free gift because our salvation, S-Factor, is the most important thing in life. Finally after reading this book, I encourage you to PRAY and ask yourself this critical question, "Once I accept Christ's gift of salvation, what does God want me to do next?"

# Epilogue: A Pastor's Perspective

Salvation is not one factor to be considered among other factors of equal importance. Rather, salvation is the primary purpose which takes precedence over every other idea, interest, or objective known to humanity. The destiny of humanity, for weal or for woe, hinges upon the S-Factor!

In the words of the song, "The theme of the Bible is Jesus, and how He died to save men," Jesus and His salvation is the central message of the entire Bible (John 5:39)! The whole Bible is about salvation—S-Factor. The message of salvation was first proclaimed in Eden to Adam and Eve (Genesis 3:15). This message has been repeated from age to age and from generation to generation.

When the message of salvation has been preached in all the world, then the end will come (Matthew 24:14). And even when Jesus comes again, and the faithful are honored with a home in heaven, salvation—S-Factor—will be the science and song of the redeemed! Salvation is the main thing.

The message of salvation is not only the main thing, it is also the best thing. Salvation is the good news that every human heart is hoping to hear. Our fear and doubt, our guilt and shame yearn for the assurance of acceptance with God. This yearning is answered in the very name of Jesus. "Jehovah is salvation," is the Hebrew meaning of the name Jesus. Oh, how sweet the name of Jesus sounds in a believer's ear—Jesus saves! Jesus saves!

I have heard this joyful sound myself. I recall being a seminary student and earnestly wanting to understand how salvation works and (more importantly) to have the assurance that it was working for me. I remember reading what Paul says about God's gracious salvation in Titus 3:5: "Not by works of righteousness which we have done, but according to his mercy he saved us." And if that were not enough, all the hope I needed was found in the declaration of Romans 4:5 that God "justifies the ungodly" who believe in Him. The good news of the S-Factor brought peace to my heart! I pray that as you read this book, S-FACTOR, it did the same for you.

### Pastor Donald C. McKinnie, Jr., DMin.
*Pastor McKinnie is an ordained minister and urban ministry practitioner. He pastors two churches in central Pennsylvania, where he lives with his incredible wife, Lahai, and three amazing children.*

*The End*

**S-Factor**

# *Overcomer (Book One) Excerpt: Teacup Prayer*

I could barely breathe and pain raced through my body. It felt as if someone was jumping up and down on my heart and lungs in concrete spiked shoes. I listened on the prayer line as my sisters and brothers in Christ discussed the Word of God and rejoiced in His glory. After discussing various Scriptures, it was time for prayer.

I did not feel like praying, but I have learned that whenever I do not feel like praying, I should pray. I offered to pray. As I opened my mouth, the sadness in my heart poured out over the phone line. After the prayer conference call ended, I stood in my kitchen for several minutes trying to garner enough strength to take the next steps and get ready for the day.

I did not want to go to work. I only wanted to curl up in bed and sleep the day away. My job

**Bridgette Bastien**

had become stressful, the team despondent, and the environment so cutthroat and toxic that I wanted to be anywhere else but work. For the past several months, I had been working longer hours, spending less and less time with my family, and missing out on special moments with my children. I felt like I was in quicksand grasping at branches and struggling to make it out alive.

The phone ringing pulled me from my trance and day-mare about work. I answered the it, and almost immediately, I recognized the voice on the other end of the line. It was a member of our prayer group. I barely said hello when my church sister said, "I could hear the sadness in your voice as you prayed this morning. I had to call you before you left for work."

Tears started flowing from my eyes and the only words I could say were, "Thank you." My heart filled with both appreciation and sadness. She then said, "Before I pray, do you mind if I share this story with you? The story is about a

## S-Factor

teacup. It is by an unknown author and it goes like this:

> There was a couple who used to go to England to shop. They both liked antiques and pottery (especially teacups). This was their twenty-fifth wedding anniversary so they decided to go shopping. In this quaint shop, they saw a beautiful teacup set sitting on a velvet cloth on the top shelf. They said to the shopkeeper, "May we see that? We've never seen one quite so beautiful."
>
> As the lady handed it to them, suddenly the teacup spoke. "You don't understand," it said. "I haven't always been a teacup. There was a time when I was a lump of red clay. My master took me, rolled me, and patted me over and over until I yelled out, 'Let me alone,' but he only smiled and said, 'Not yet.'

**Bridgette Bastien**

"I was placed on a spinning wheel," the cup said, "and suddenly I was spun around and around and around. 'Stop it! I'm getting dizzy!' I screamed. But the master only nodded and said, 'Not yet.' He then put me in the oven.

I never felt such heat! I wondered why he wanted to burn me, and I yelled and knocked at the door. I could see him through the opening, and I could read his lips as He shook his head and said, 'Not yet.' Finally, the door opened, he put me on the shelf, and I began to cool down.

'There, that's better,' I said. And he brushed and painted me all over. The fumes were horrible. I thought I would gag. 'Stop it, stop it!' I cried. He only nodded, 'Not yet.' Then suddenly he put me back into the oven.

## S-Factor

It was not like the first one. This was twice as hot, and I knew I would suffocate. I begged. I pleaded. I screamed. I cried. All the time I could see him through the opening, nodding his head saying, 'Not yet...'

**Bridgette Bastien**

# *Preview of Book Three: Angel on the Plane*

Emotionally and physically drained, I plopped down in my seat on the Boeing 777 plane. My daughters and I were headed home from London by way of Ireland. Both girls were safely tucked into their seats and fully equipped with their blankets, books, electronics, and travel toys. I was just about to breathe a sigh of relief when I realized the three of us were sitting in a row with four seats. This meant that my youngest daughter would be next to a complete stranger for the seven-hour flight.

My heart skipped a beat as I scanned our co-passenger from head to toe. He was a tall gentleman in his mid-thirties. His colorful, casual shirt contrasted with his khaki dress pants. My anxiety level went from zero to a hundred, although there was nothing physically appalling about him. His long dark brown hair was wildly

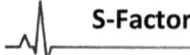 **S-Factor**

tucked into a ponytail and his rugged beard made him look like someone from the 1960s.

As I looked him over and reflected on the hellish morning we had—my stranger danger radar went on high alert. I wouldn't have trusted anyone that afternoon based on the drama and trauma we experienced earlier in the day. Almost everything had gone wrong that morning. Why would this flight be any different?

I was frustrated and had become so worked up that I didn't realize we were sitting next to an angel. His halo and wings weren't immediately visible to me, but maybe I was just too distraught to notice them. You would've overlooked his angelic glow too, if you went through what we did that morning.

What was supposed to be an uneventful trip back home turned into the worst travel experience I've had in my entire life. Just imagine, leaving the house at 4 a.m., skipping breakfast, driving two hours to the airport with

**Bridgette Bastien**

two young kids, shuttling back and forth several times to different terminals within the Heathrow airport, and having an angry cab driver throw your five bags out of his taxi onto the curb.

All this happened before 8 a.m., and it wasn't even the worst part of the day. There was more madness and misfortune even after I burst into tears at the security checkpoint. (Yes, I had a major melt-down at security and will give the juicy details a bit later.)

Sobbing uncontrollably in front of my daughters and other travelers, I began to ponder LIFE. I find it ironic that some of my most unforgettable life lessons have been learned during inconvenient and chaotic times. I wiped away my tears, while wondering why the sweetest moments often turn into sour memories.

I cringed knowing that I had scared my daughters by breaking down in public. I tried my best, but the floodgates had already broken

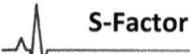 S-Factor

open. I couldn't hold back the anger and tears that rushed from my soul as rivers of water.

During our travel fiasco, I never thought to pray. I was so wound up that I couldn't find the words. I thought I had everything under control and had the ideal travel plan. When things went haywire, I began questioning all the decisions I had made that morning, like skipping breakfast and getting in a cab with an irate driver.

Three hours later, I still hadn't fed my daughters and I felt like the worst mother ever. In this frame of mind, it's no surprise that I didn't recognize the angel on the plane sitting in our row. Recognizing the angel was the climax of our long trip home. Once that happened, I had to admit that LIFE is full of surprises.

Book three in the Prayer Saved My Life (PSML) Series will also be filled with surprises!

**COMING SOON - BOOK THREE!**

## About the Author

*Bridgette Bastien* is a prayer enthusiast and the author of the *Prayer Saved My Life* Series. Writing a book was never on her bucket list until she was snatched from the jaws of death. After going through that experience, she had a reignited, burning desire to share the transformational power of prayer and to share the saving grace of God with others. She feasts on the Bible and, according to her daughters, "has playdates with her prayer group three times per day."

Bastien has written two books, OVERCOMER and S-FACTOR, and she has published several children's books written by her daughters. She

## S-Factor

was a research chemist early in her career, holds a master's degree in Strategy and Marketing from the Wharton School of Business—University of Pennsylvania, and is now a Marketing Professional. Bastien lives in Massachusetts with her family. She loves traveling the world, eating spicy foods, and basking in the warmth of her family and friends' love.

Learn more on the PSML website and follow Bastien on social media:

- www.prayersavedmylife.com
- Facebook.com/prayersavedmylife
- Instagram.com/prayersavedmylife
- Twitter.com/prayersavedmy

**Bridgette Bastien**

## *Special thanks to my Editors:*

### *Debra Banks Cuadro* holds a B.A. in

Communication and is a published author with more than 25 years of experience in writing featured articles, news stories, and personal interest pieces for faith-based magazines. She is currently the associate director of communication for the Atlantic Union Conference. She lives with her family in Massachusetts. Her favorite scripture is Psalms 37:5: *"Commit your way to the Lord, trust also in Him, and He shall bring it to pass."* Cuadro says, "Salvation is unmerited favor from a loving Savior who sees more in me than I see in myself."

### *Kerrie Howard* is a dedicated

pastor's wife, homeschool teacher, and freelance editor. She holds a bachelor's degree in English from Worcester State University and a master's degree in Publishing from The George Washington University. Above all, her desire is to

**S-Factor**

serve her Lord and Savior, Jesus Christ, in everything that she does. Kerrie clings to the scripture that says: "Be still and know that I am God" (Psalm 46:10). She has found peace in the stillness and joy in the simplicities of life. Howard says, "Salvation is LIFE."

**Bridgette Bastien**

## *Eternally grateful for the Writing with Purpose Group:*

*Fiona Harewood* is a published author of several books and a motivational speaker. Her book—*I Did It, You Can, Too!* is part of the Philadelphia School District's summer reading list. Harewood has a master's degree in public policy from Drexel University and works with the federal government. She lives in Philadelphia with her family and is a member of Mizpah SDA Church.

Harewood has a passion for writing, working with children, and using her gifts to glorify God. She often reflects on Proverbs 31:30, which says, *"Charm is deceitful and beauty is passing, but a woman who fears the Lord, she shall be praised.* Harewood says, "Salvation is what a wonderful Savior gave me when He hung on Calvary!"

## S-Factor

*Nathan Stephens* is an innovative professional who delivers a comprehensive portfolio of services and results-oriented solutions designed to help align people, processes, and technology. With 20+ years of experience in professional IT service delivery, Nathan works closely with CIOs and IT Executives in various organizations. He is a customer advocate throughout all aspects of the customer lifecycle supported by Lean Six Sigma methodologies.

As a member of the Writing with Purpose Group, Nathan has been critical to the completion and publication of this book. He lives in the United Arab Emirates with his wonderful wife and is currently writing his first book. Stephens says, "Salvation is an everlasting peace. Even though I may sin, I will be saved by the grace of God."

**Bridgette Bastien**

Prayer Can **SAVE** Your Life

www.ingramcontent.com/pod-product-compliance
Lightning Source LLC
Chambersburg PA
CBHW070656100426
42735CB00039B/2157